patternless
SEWING MODstyle

Patty Prann Young

24 Garments for Women and Girls

Just Measure, Cut & Sew for the Perfect Fit!

stash BOOKS.

an imprint of C&T Publishing

Publisher: Amy Marson

Creative Director: Gailen Runge

Editor: Karla Menaugh

Technical Editor: Alison M. Schmidt

Cover/Book Design and
Style Photography: Page + Pixel

Production Coordinator:
Freesia Pearson Blizard

Production Editor:
Alice Mace Nakanishi

Illustrator: Patty Prann Young

Photo Assistant: Sarah Frost

Instructional photography
by Diane Pedersen, unless
otherwise noted

Published by Stash Books, an imprint of C&T Publishing, Inc., P.O. Box 1456,
Lafayette, CA 94549

Library of Congress Cataloging-in-Publication Data

Names: Young, Patty Prann, 1971- author.

Title: Patternless sewing mod style : just measure, cut & sew for the perfect
fit!--24 garments for women and girls / Patty Prann Young.

Description: Lafayette, California : C&T Publishing, 2016.

Identifiers: LCCN 2015044371 | ISBN 9781617451805 (soft cover)

Subjects: LCSH: Dressmaking--Pattern design. | Dressmaking. | Fashion
design. | Sewing. | Machine sewing.

Classification: LCC TT520 .Y68 2016 | DDC 646.4--dc23

LC record available at http://lccn.loc.gov/2015044371

Printed in the China

10 9 8 7 6 5 4 3 2 1

Acknowledgments

I owe my immediate family—namely, my dear husband, Jon, and my two sweet daughters, Sophie and Sydney—a huge thank-you (with an added heartfelt apology) for putting up with my absence these past few months while I worked on this book. Your love, encouragement, and understanding fueled me through those long work days and sleepless nights. I love you with all my heart!

The sample projects you see in the pages of this book were sewn by my two interns extraordinaire, Megan Dowling and Kait Lorenz, and for that I will be eternally grateful. These two girls came in eager to tackle a new project each day with a smile on their faces and a positive attitude. You can't put a price on that.

The textiles, notions, and trims we used in all the projects in this book were graciously contributed by Riley Blake Designs, Jo-Ann Fabric and Craft Stores, and Shannon Fabrics. Thank you, from the bottom of my heart, to these three companies for being just as excited about this book as I am, and sending me boxes upon boxes of gorgeous materials to use in these projects.

Last, but certainly not least, I would like to thank a couple of very special women from C&T Publishing. This book would not have been possible without the support, encouragement, and friendship of my acquisitions editor and dearest friend, Roxane Cerda. Thank you for always believing in me! Also, words cannot express my gratitude to my developmental editor, Karla Menaugh, for her patience, kind words, and expertise in getting this book to where it is today. Lastly, to the graphic designers, photographers, and models, thank you from the bottom of my heart for making me look good.

Contents

*I dedicate this book to my
sweet mom, Maria Prann
(a.k.a. "Mami"), from whom
I inherited my desire to
create something new
every day.*

Introduction

It may seem odd for a sewing pattern designer to write a book about patternless sewing. For the past eight years I have designed patterns for everything from girls' dresses to women's tops to purses and even quilts. Some are extremely complicated, using unusually shaped sleeves or bodice pieces. But others just use straight cuts of fabric, which are then gathered, pleated, or folded into new shapes. The new shapes are often sewn onto other straight cuts of fabric to form a finished garment. These simpler designs are the types of projects that this book is all about.

You can start with simple dresses that are sewn from a single cut of fabric, but by the end of this book you will be sewing runway-worthy garments that are not only stylish but also a perfect fit because they are made based on your own body measurements.

People come in all shapes and sizes. Maybe you're extra petite, or maybe you have a full bustline; maybe you have a long torso but short legs … or vice versa. Not all of us are shaped like supermodels. It's challenging to find not only ready-to-wear garments but also sewing patterns that fit us perfectly. Often, we buy a sewing pattern hoping that the end result will make us look like the cover model, but in the end we've made so many alterations that we might as well have drafted our own pattern.

This is where *Patternless Sewing Mod Style* comes in. I have designed 24 easy-to-sew projects that span all seasons and are made based on your own body measurements for a perfect fit every time. Embellish and add flair to all your base garments with eight predesigned add-on pieces—various pocket styles, belts, hem ruffles, and bands—and you can easily create a large wardrobe of custom-fitted pieces for yourself or your child. So let's get started!

Taking Your Measurements

The most important goal, when sewing for yourself or others, is to have a perfect fit. You will achieve this by jotting down a set of body measurements—for yourself, your kids, or your friends—that you can easily refer to while working on these projects.

Use a flexible tape measure and refer to the descriptions. Use the fill-in chart to jot down your measurements in pencil, so you can easily update them later.

If you need your own measurements, it is easier to have someone else do the measuring for you.

WOMAN/TEEN

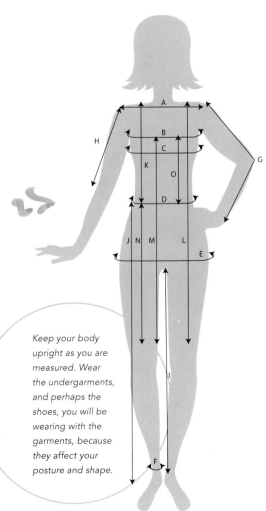

Keep your body upright as you are measured. Wear the undergarments, and perhaps the shoes, you will be wearing with the garments, because they affect your posture and shape.

A = Shoulder Width   Using a favorite shirt that fits you perfectly, measure from shoulder seam to shoulder seam across the back.

B = Upper Bust   All the way around your body just under your armpit, where a strapless dress would start.

C = Full Bust   All the way around your body at the fullest part of your bust and the widest part of your back. Don't let the tape measure sag in the back.

D = Waist   All the way around your body at your natural waistline (the narrowest part).

E = Hips   All the way around your body at the widest part of your hip. This is usually about 7″–9″ below your natural waist. Keep the tape measure level all the way around.

F = Ankle   All the way around your ankle.

G = Arm Length   From your shoulder seam (A) all the way down to 1″ past your wrist. Bend your elbow slightly when you measure.

H = Elbow Length   From your shoulder seam (A) down to your elbow.

I = Inseam   From your crotch down to your ankle. Be sure to keep your leg fully extended and straight, or measure a favorite pair of pants.

J = Outseam   This is essentially your finished pant length. Measure from your natural waist to 1″ below your ankle down your side, or measure a favorite pair of pants along the outer side seam.

K = Bodice Length   From the top of your shoulder down to your natural waistline (or below if you like longer shirts).

L = Dress Length   From the top of your shoulder down to where you would like your dresses to fall. You can always adjust this length for a longer or shorter style.

M = Strapless Dress Length (*or any dress with shoulder straps and a bodice that goes straight across the bust*)   From your Upper Bust (B) down to where you would like your dresses to fall.

N = Skirt Length   From your natural waist down to where you would like your skirts to fall. You can always adjust this length later for a longer or shorter style.

O = Strapless Blouse Length   From your Upper Bust (B) down to where you would like your tops to fall.

MY MEASUREMENTS
(WOMAN/TEEN)

NAME

A	4 4	I	
B		J	
C		K	
D		L	
E		M	
F		N	
G		O	
H			

Taking Your Child's Measurements

Because kids' bodies are shaped differently than women's, use a different chart to record their numbers. If your girl has already started developing, use the Woman/Teen chart (page 5).

Use a flexible tape measure and refer to the descriptions for how to take each body measurement.

Use the fill-in chart to jot down her measurements in pencil, so you can easily update them as she grows.

GIRL/TWEEN

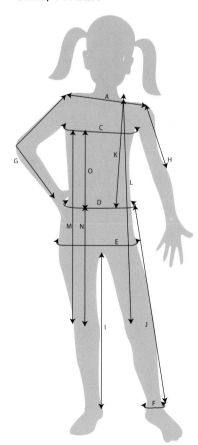

A = Shoulder Width   From shoulder to shoulder, across the back, right where the seams will fall on a shirt.

B has been deliberately skipped because most Girls'/Tweens' sizes have the same measurement for Upper Bust and Chest/Bust. If your girl has a larger Chest/Bust than Upper Bust, use the Woman/Teen measurement chart.

C = Chest   All the way around her chest, just under her armpit, where a sleeveless dress would start.

D = Waist   All the way around her body at the waistline.

E = Hips   All the way around her body at the widest part of her hip. Keep your tape measure level all the way around.

F = Ankle   All the way around her ankle.

G = Arm Length   From her shoulder seam (A) down to ½˝ past her wrist. Make sure her arm is slightly bent at the elbow.

H = Elbow Length   From her shoulder seam (A) down to her elbow.

I = Inseam   From her crotch down to her ankle. Make sure her leg is fully extended and straight.

J = Outseam   This is essentially her full finished pant length. Measure from her natural waist to ½˝ below her ankle down the side, or measure a favorite pair of her pants along the outer side seam.

K = Bodice Length   From the top of her shoulder to her waistline.

L = Dress Length   From the top of her shoulder to where you would like her dresses to fall. You can always adjust this length for a longer or shorter style.

M = Strapless Dress Length (*or any dress with shoulder straps and a bodice that goes straight across the bust*)   From her chest (under armpits) down to where you would like her dresses to fall.

N = Skirt Length   From her waist down to where you would like her skirts to fall. You can always adjust this length for a longer or shorter style.

O = Strapless Blouse Length   From her chest (under armpits) down to where you would like her tops to fall.

MY MEASUREMENTS (GIRL/TWEEN)

NAME
A
C
D
E
F
G
H
I
J
K
L
M
N
O

Know Your Fabrics

The two most common types of clothing textiles are wovens and knits. Each project in this book will have a list of suggested fabrics. Sometimes the project can be made from either wovens or knits, and sometimes it can be made from only knits or only wovens. It is very important to follow the fabric recommendations because not all garments work well with all types of fabrics.

Let's go through some basic information on how woven and knit fabrics are created. This will help you understand why a certain fabric type is recommended over another in each project.

WOVENS   In woven fabrics, two or more sets of threads are interlaced (woven) at right angles to each other, similar to a basket-weave process. During the weaving process, typically done on a commercial loom, the vertical threads (called warp threads) are held in place, while the horizontal threads (called weft threads) are woven under and over the warp threads to create the desired effect. Woven fabrics generally do not stretch unless some spandex has been added among the fibers during the weaving process. However, cutting woven fabrics on the bias (at a 45° angle, instead of parallel to the selvage) will add some stretch. Examples of woven fabrics are (among others) quilting cotton, shirting, suiting, lawn, voile, twill, canvas, denim, and corduroy.

Woven fabric

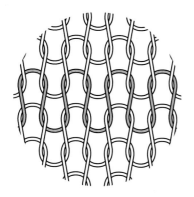

Weft-knitted fabric

Warp-knitted fabric

KNITS These fabrics are made by interconnecting loops of yarns, using the knit and purl stitches. Knit fabrics are created on a knitting machine, which pulls the yarns through the loops of the previous row of yarn to create a new row. There are weft-knitted fabrics, in which the yarns are inserted in a horizontal or weft direction, and there are warp-knitted fabrics, in which the yarn is inserted in the warp or vertical direction. Depending on how these yarns are looped, knit fabrics can have either two-way stretch, stretching sideways only, or four-way stretch, stretching both horizontally and vertically. Always cut knit fabric so that the maximum stretch goes horizontally across your body, never vertically. On fabrics with four-way stretch, you should always cut pieces so that the length is parallel to the selvage. Examples of knit fabrics are (among others) jersey, interlock, and rib knit.

In addition to knowing whether a fabric is woven or knit, you also need to be aware of other properties in the fabric you choose, such as thickness, fiber content, wrinkle resistance, stretch, drape, nap, and more.

DRAPE Refers to the way a fabric hangs on your body or on a dress form. Stiffer or thicker fabrics generally have less drape than thinner fabrics. If you will be sewing a flowy dress or skirt, you will want fabrics with greater drape because they will hug your body and move with ease. When you are making dress pants, structured jackets, or pleated skirts, you will have better results with less drapey fabrics because they will hold their shape better.

NAP Refers to the fuzzy surface on certain types of fabrics such as velvet, velveteen, velour, or corduroy. Typically nap has a right and wrong direction. When constructing garments with these types of fabrics, pay attention to the direction of the nap so it doesn't end up upside down. The easiest way to tell the right direction of the nap is by running your hands on the surface of the fabric. The nap will feel softer in the right direction and rougher in the wrong direction. Always sew with the direction of the nap pointing down.

FIBER CONTENT   Refers to the composition of the yarn or threads used in the fabric. Knowing the fiber content is important because it will affect the appearance, comfort, durability, and care (washing/drying instructions). Natural fibers can be plant-based, like cotton, hemp, or bamboo, or animal-based, like wool, silk, or angora. Synthetic fibers are man-made materials like acrylic, rayon, polyester, nylon, and spandex (Lycra). There are also synthetic blend fabrics, such as poly/cotton. When you shop for fabric, look for the fiber content on a label on the side of the bolt. Fibers present in quantities greater than 1% must be labeled by percentage as a required component of the product's label.

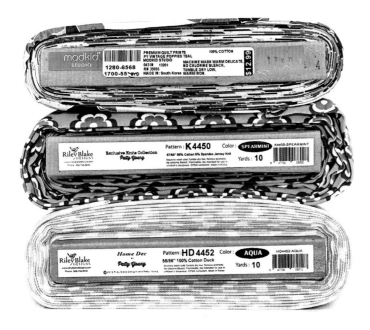

STRETCH   On fabrics with stretch, it is important to know not only whether the fabric has a two-way stretch (stretches sideways only) or a four-way stretch (stretches in all directions), but also its recovery factor. Refer to the stretch gauge to determine the amount of stretch in your fabric. To do this, fold an 8″-wide piece of knit fabric in half to get a 4″-wide piece, with the maximum stretch going from side to side along the fold. Place the folded fabric in the pink area, and then pull the edge without distorting it. Hold the edge against the chart to determine the percentage of stretch. If the pattern or project requires a fabric with stretch, look for knits with at least 25% stretch and excellent recovery (fabric bounces back to its original 4″ width).

STRETCH
GAUGE

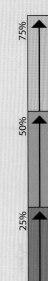

75%

50%

25%

4″ OF FOLDED FABRIC

The following types of fabrics can be used in this book's projects:

BROADCLOTH A woven fabric with a tight weave. Can be used for skirts, blouses, dresses, and summer clothing that requires a fair amount of structure, since it does not drape well.

CANVAS A heavy, textured fabric. Often used for home decor projects and bags/totes. Can also be used for capes or coats, but needs to be lined because the wrong side of the fabric can be rough and scratchy.

CHIFFON A drapeable, sheer fabric made from silk or polyester. It has a smooth, lustrous surface, which makes it perfect for wrap skirts, beach cover-ups, and scarves.

CORDUROY A bottom-weight, ridged fabric with visible nap/pile, also known as *wales*. Corduroys come in all thicknesses and the wales can be wide or narrow. Can be used for skirts, capes, coats, and other garments that require structure.

CREPE A lightweight fabric with a crinkled surface. Can be used for skirts, dresses, and tops.

DENIM A rugged cotton twill fabric with parallel diagonal ridges. It's generally thick and stiff, and should be used only for projects that require structure, such as pants, jackets, or non-flowy skirts.

DOUBLE KNIT A thick and stable knit fabric that is two-faced, which means the back and front look exactly the same. Use on projects that require both stretch and structure. Not recommended for projects that require shirring, since the thickness will prevent the fabric from gathering as much as needed.

EYELET A lightweight woven fabric most commonly made of cotton but also sometimes from silk or synthetic fibers. It is characterized by small holes throughout, finished with stitching around the edges. It is lightweight enough to be used for beach cover-ups, summer tops, skirts, and dresses.

FLEECE A soft fabric with deep pile usually made of synthetic fibers. It may or may not contain stretch, depending on its spandex content. Perfect for outerwear, such as all the capes and capelets in this book.

GEORGETTE A drapeable, sheer fabric similar to chiffon but slightly heavier and less sheer, with a slight surface texture. Perfect for wrap skirts, beach cover-ups, and scarves.

INTERLOCK A knit fabric that is the same on both sides and typically has only two-way stretch. It is thicker and more stable than jersey, but it pills more easily. Cut edges lie flat. Perfect for tops, dresses, and skirts.

JERSEY A knit fabric with either two-way or four-way stretch. The cut edges will curl. Does not fray. Perfect for tops, dresses, and skirts.

LAWN A lightweight woven fabric primarily made of linen or cotton. It is made with very fine thread in a high thread count, which creates a smooth, untextured surface. Perfect for sundresses and lightweight tops.

ORGANZA   A crisp, very sheer fabric usually made from silk, nylon, or polyester yarns. Organza differs from chiffon and georgette in that it is not drapeable at all, so it usually stands away from the body when worn.

POPLIN   A medium-weight woven fabric with a very finely ribbed surface. Can be 100% cotton or a poly/cotton blend. Perfect for structured skirts, pants, and coats, and capes.

RIB KNIT   A knit fabric with visible ridges on both sides. It is thick and stable with lots of stretch and great recovery, which makes it perfect for yoga waistbands and pant cuffs, like those on our Harem Pants (page 59).

SATIN   A smooth and soft-to-the-touch woven fabric with a high amount of sheen. Can be stretchy with the addition of spandex. Perfect for evening wear.

TERRY   Also called terry cloth, a woven fabric with looped pile on both sides. Because it is very absorbent, it is perfect not only for towels but also for bathrobes and swim cover-ups. There is also stretch terry, a knit fabric with no pile on the wrong side.

TULLE   A thin, stiff, fine netting made from silk, nylon, or rayon. We use it for our version of the tutu, Pixie Skirt (page 95).

TWEED   A medium- to heavyweight woolen fabric. It is often characterized by a chevron or herringbone pattern on the surface. It is perfect for capes, capelets, and vests.

TWILL   A medium- to heavyweight woven fabric with diagonal ridges. Perfect for all projects that require structure and no stretch.

VELOUR   A soft fabric with a thick nap, similar to velvet. It is most commonly a knit fabric but also exists as a woven. Some velour has a small percentage of spandex woven into the fibers, making it even more stretchy. Perfect for outerwear projects such as capes, capelets, cloaks, vests, jackets, and shoulder wraps.

VELVET   A soft, lush fabric primarily made of silk, rayon, or polyester. It has a longer pile than both velour and velveteen, and often is softer and shinier. Perfect for outerwear projects such as capes, capelets, cloaks, vests, jackets, and shoulder wraps.

VELVETEEN   A woven fabric with short pile. It is stiffer than velvet and closely related to corduroy but without the wales.

VOILE   A lightweight, breathable fabric usually made from cottons or cotton blends. It has a moderate amount of drape, like chiffon and georgette, but is less sheer. Perfect for summer dresses, skirts, and tops. It shirrs like a dream!

Before
You Begin

Now that you know everything you ever wanted to know about fabrics, it is time to gather all the tools you'll need for drafting your own pattern and sewing your garment.

At the beginning of each project, I will give you a "formula," so to speak. It will generally start with a square or rectangle, cut based on your body measurements (see Taking Your Measurements, page 5, or Taking Your Child's Measurements, page 6). You will subcut this square or rectangle into either smaller rectangles or other geometric shapes, such as a triangle or a circle.

If you are the cautious type, you may cut all these shapes out of paper first, essentially creating a paper pattern, which you can reuse to make that same garment again.

Tools for Pattern Drafting

LARGE SHEETS OF PAPER You can use anything from newsprint to butcher's paper to printer paper taped together to form larger sheets. However, if you are serious about the craft, a few products are specifically designed for pattern drafting.

- Pattern tracing paper is smooth and opaque, and comes in rolls 21″ × 77 yards. Available online through several sources for $7–$8 per roll.

- Swedish Tracing Paper is what European dressmakers use to make their "muslins." It is sewable and washable, which is a plus. Comes in rolls 29″ × 10 yards and retails for about $15 online.

- Pellon 830 Easy Pattern is a lightweight but strong, nonfusible, nonwoven interfacing that is designed for use in pattern drafting and tracing. It is perfect for altering, duplicating, and tracing patterns. It is safe for inkjet printers, making it ideal for printing pattern pieces for extended use. It is available 45″ wide on 10-yard bolts, retails for $2–$3 per yard, and can be purchased at Jo-Ann Fabric and Craft Stores or other fabric stores.

- Medical pattern paper is what doctors use on their exam tables, but it happens to be perfect for pattern drafting too! Find it on Amazon in rolls 21″ × 225 feet for only $10–$12.

RULERS The longer the better in this case, because often you will need to make long marks on your paper or fabric, and it is cumbersome to try to do this with a short ruler. I love using my 6″ × 24″ nonslip quilter's ruler for pattern drafting,

and these are also available up to 36″ long! For curved lines, a set of French curves is ideal, but for most of the projects in this book that require curved lines, you can use a small or large dinner plate as a template.

FLEXIBLE MEASURING TAPE This is to measure yourself or your model, not for transferring measurements to the paper: you will not get a straight line with a flexible measuring tape.

MARKING TOOLS For marking on paper you can use just about anything—pencils, pens, markers. For marking on fabric, you will need a water-soluble fabric marker (disappearing-ink pen) or chalk pencil.

PAPER SCISSORS You may know this already, but in case you don't—never, ever use your fabric scissors to cut paper! The paper will dull the blade, and in turn a dull blade will damage the fabric. If your fabric scissors look similar to your paper scissors, tie a pretty ribbon in the handle of your fabric scissors to tell them apart.

CALCULATOR Even though you've already written down all of your body measurements, you will still need to add ease on some garments or divide these measurements in half for others, or even find the radius of a circle based on its circumference (no joke!). Unless you are a math whiz, it is helpful to have a calculator nearby to help with these equations.

If you are the adventurous type and want to go straight to cutting your fabric instead of making a pattern first, you may skip most of the items mentioned above, except for the calculator, the ruler, the flexible measuring tape, and the fabric markers. You will need those tools regardless.

Tools for Sewing

SEWING MACHINE   It does not have to be a fancy or expensive one. As long as it can do a straight stitch and a zigzag stitch, you will be able to tackle each and every project in this book … even the ones with buttonholes!

SERGER   It is not necessary but oh, so nice to have. If you want your garments to have a nice finished edge with an overlocked seam, this is the machine you need. But you can always finish your seams with a wide zigzag stitch.

THREAD IN COORDINATING COLORS   I prefer to use polyester or poly/cotton threads for garment construction because they are stronger than their 100% cotton counterparts. Also, they will give a little with the seams, which is something you want, especially if you are sewing with knit fabrics.

MACHINE NEEDLES   You may want to stock up on a variety of machine sewing needles. You will need a different one for each type of fabric. You'll need these for the projects in this book:

- *Universal needles:* For most woven light- to medium-weight fabrics

- *Ballpoint needles:* For most knit fabrics

- *Stretch needles:* For swimwear fabrics or other stretch fabrics with high Lycra content

- *Denim needles:* For denim, canvas, twill, and other thick woven fabrics

GOOD-QUALITY FABRIC SCISSORS   Don't skimp on these! Your fingers and your fabric will thank you later.

TURNING TOOLS   There are many tools on the market that help you turn skinny straps, belts, or loops right side out, but my favorite turning tool is a *hemostat*, also called *forceps* or a *clamp*. You can buy these online. I prefer them because they don't pierce the fabric and they clamp on tightly, so you can pull without the fear that the fabric will come apart. You can find these on the Internet for about $7, and you can sometimes find them on the tool tables at craft shows for even less.

BODKIN OR SAFETY PINS OF VARIOUS SIZES   These are used for inserting elastic or drawstrings through casings.

WATER-SOLUBLE FABRIC MARKER OR CHALK PENCIL   Used to transfer pattern markings (notches, button or pocket positioning, and so on) to the fabric. Disappearing ink pens are also wonderful for this purpose, but always test them first on a scrap of the fabric you plan to use. Some marks can be made permanent by the heat of an iron.

SEAM AND HEM GAUGES   To help you get that perfectly even hem.

EXTRA BOBBINS   Keep them loaded with your favorite thread colors, and load one with elastic thread for shirring.

SEAM RIPPER   A necessary evil! Alex Anderson's 4-in-1 Essential Sewing Tool has a seam ripper, a pointed wooden end cap for turning bias tubes, a stiletto, and a flat-ended presser cap.

When in Doubt, Make a Muslin!

If you are not interested in drafting a paper pattern but are a bit unsure as to whether the garment will fit, drape, and look as good as you want it to, make a muslin first. A muslin is a test garment, like a mock-up or rough draft, made out of any inexpensive fabric that you may have around the house. You can use actual muslin fabric (a very inexpensive unbleached cotton material found in most fabric stores) or you can use an old bed sheet or even an old piece of clothing that you've cut up.

To make a muslin, cut the project out and sew it as instructed. It will go faster than you think because you don't need to finish the seams or add buttons or interfacing or any of those extras that add a professional touch to a finished garment. You can even use a basting stitch to make the sewing process go extra fast. Try the muslin on and adjust here and there for a perfect fit. You can use a fabric marker to make notes right on the muslin, such as "Add more ease here," "Shorten hem by an inch," and so on.

You can make alterations right on the muslin and check again for fit. Or, if you're feeling confident enough, you can transfer your alterations right onto your pretty fabric and sew your final garment.

Now that you've learned all about fabric types, pattern-making tools, and sewing tools, it is time to start sewing!

Shirr Magic

If you've never tried shirring before, you're in for a treat!

I love shirring because it always makes a perfectly fitted garment no matter how you cut the fabric. Not only will the fit be spot-on, but it will also be one of the most comfortable pieces of clothing you'll ever own, because it will move with you and adjust to your body position. The garment will be as comfy when you're sitting down as when you're walking around. Plus, shirring adds great texture to your fabric ... and it's fun to do!

If you've never tried shirring before, you're in for a treat!

All you'll need is a spool of elastic thread. My favorite brand is Stretchrite, but there are a few other brands you could try. At most fabric stores you can find elastic thread in only white or black, but online you can find it in other colors. You'll also need regular sewing thread for your needle. I prefer to use polyester or a poly/cotton blend thread because it is more durable and stretches more with the fabric than 100% cotton threads. You do not need any special needles for shirring. However, use a ballpoint needle when shirring knit fabrics, so you don't leave any large holes in the fabric.

Let's Get Started!

1. Wind elastic thread onto your bobbin by hand using a steady rhythm, not too tight and not too loose. Practice makes perfect! Use regular thread for the top in a color that matches your fabric or is the least noticeable. Use your longest machine stitch and regular tension.

NOTE

If you've never shirred before, practice on a scrap of fabric first. Every machine is different, so play with your stitch length and tension until you get it just right. Sew at least three or four rows of shirring on your practice piece to get the feel of it. The fabric should gather up nicely and you should be able to stretch it back to its original width without the threads snapping.

2. Place your fabric right side up on the machine so that the elastic thread will be on the inside (wrong side) of your garment. Use your machine's presser foot as a width guide by placing the foot's right edge up against the edge of the fabric, seam, casing, or whatever element you have chosen as the outer edge of the shirring. The first row of shirring will be ¼″ to ⅜″ away, depending on the width of your standard presser foot. Backstitch a couple of times at the beginning to secure the threads, and then straight stitch all the way from side to side. When you reach the end, backstitch again to secure threads, and then lift the presser foot, turn the fabric 90°, and take a couple of stitches vertically, parallel to the side seam. Turn the fabric another 90°, aligning the left edge of the presser foot with the first row of shirring (so you are now parallel to your first shirred row), and begin stitching again.

Wrong side

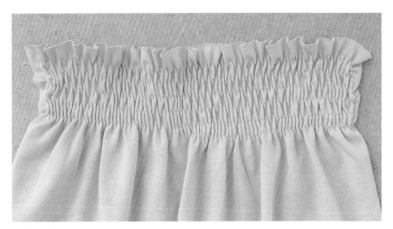

Right side

3. Repeat Step 2 to continue stitching the shirring rows ¼″–⅜″ apart, using the edge of your presser foot as a guide to keep them evenly spaced. You won't see the fabric begin to pucker until you've stitched 3 or more rows.

4. When you've finished shirring, backstitch a couple of times to secure the elastic thread. Also, leave some long thread tails and tie them off by hand. Don't worry if you think the fabric did not gather as much as you expected it to. I'll show you a little trick I've learned along the way:

After (and only after) the entire shirring portion of your garment is complete, remove the fabric from the machine and shoot it with a little bit of steam from your steam iron. Don't be afraid to get up close and personal! The steam won't hurt the garment, and you'll see the fabric gather up like magic right in front of your eyes!

Simple
Sundress

This Simple Sundress with added spaghetti straps and hem ruffle is made with Red Anchors knit fabric by Riley Blake Designs. Learn how to sew these items in Add-Ons (page 131).

Who would've thought that you could create such a fun and flattering dress with one piece of fabric and a roll of elastic thread? This Simple Sundress will be your go-to dress for all summertime events, whether you are attending a family barbeque or a friend's pool party.

Note variation with straps and ruffle (photo, page 19).

FABRIC AND NOTIONS

Use stretch fabrics, such as cotton interlocks, jerseys, rib knits, stretch velvet, or stretch velour, 58″/60″ wide. Avoid thicker fabrics, such as double knits, because they will be difficult to shirr. Top-weight woven fabrics, such as quilting cottons, shirtings, lawns, voiles, satins, and eyelets also work well for this style of dress. Refer to Know Your Fabrics (page 7).

The amount of fabric you need to buy will vary depending on size, dress length, and add-ons. Refer to the cutting instructions to determine the yardage. Always purchase at least ¼ yard extra to allow for fabric shrinkage.

- ½–1½ yards (depending on size) of ½″-wide knit elastic
- 1 spool of elastic thread
- Coordinating thread
- Rotary cutter and self-healing mat, or dressmaking shears
- Flexible measuring tape

CUTTING

These directions are based on fabrics at least 58″ wide. Calculate the width of your dress based on C on the measuring chart (pages 5 or 6) (for Girls/Tweens, the Chest measurement, or for Women/Teens, the Full Bust measurement). Base the length on M, the Strapless Dress Length. Grab your calculator because you will need it for this one!

1. Cut 1 dress panel, or 2 for larger sizes, following these formulas to get the size:

WIDTH: C + ⅓ of C. Round up your numbers. For example, if my Full Bust measures 40″, the width of my fabric panel will be 40″ + 14″ = 54″.

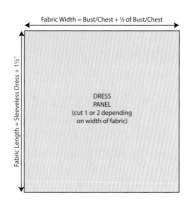

NOTE

If the total width of your dress is wider than the width of your fabric (most knits come in 58″/60″ width), divide the dress width in half, add 1″ for seam allowances, and cut 2 identical pieces.

Fabric Width = Bust/Chest + ⅓ of Bust/Chest

Fabric Length = Sleeveless Dress + 1½″

DRESS PANEL
(cut 1 or 2 depending on width of fabric)

LENGTH: Strapless Dress Length (M) + 1½″ to allow for hem and casing allowances. For example, if my Strapless Dress Length measurement is 32″, the length of my fabric will be 33½″.

2. Cut the ½″-wide elastic:

LENGTH:
 GIRLS' SIZES: C – 2″
 WOMEN'S/TEENS' SIZES: Upper Bust (B) – 2″

Assemble

All seams are ½". Backstitch at the beginning and end of all seams.

1. If you cut 2 panels for your dress, the seams will be on the sides. Place the fabric right sides together with the side seams aligned, and stitch down 1 side only. Finish the seam with a serger or a zigzag stitch and press to the side. Leave the other side open so you can shirr the garment while it is still flat.

If your dress will be made from a single panel, the seam will be in the back. No need to sew up any seams at this point; you will want to shirr the garment while the fabric is flat.

2. Serge the top edge of the dress panel or finish with a zigzag stitch. Create an elastic casing at the top of the dress panel by folding the top edge down ¾" toward the wrong side, pressing well, and then stitching along the serged/finished edge all the way across the top of the dress panel. Don't insert the elastic yet. It's much easier to do this after you shirr the top portion of the dress. **Fig. A**

3. Determine the height of the portion to be shirred by measuring from the top folded edge down. Typically, you want the shirring to cover just the chest/bust area to create an empire waist. Mark the end of the shirred portion on the right side of the fabric with a water-soluble marker, some masking tape, or a row of pins (use ballpoint pins if you are working with knit fabric).

4. Follow the shirring instructions in Shirr Magic (page 16), working with the dress panel right side up on the sewing machine so the elastic thread will be on the wrong side of your garment. Make sure the rows of shirring are as wide as your standard presser foot and the last line of stitching aligns with your mark. Shoot the shirred section with steam to gather the fabric fully.

NOTE

If you use a coverstitch machine, you don't need to serge or zigzag first. Just stitch the raw edge down after folding and pressing.

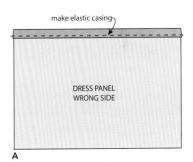

make elastic casing

DRESS PANEL
WRONG SIDE

A

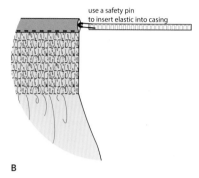

use a safety pin
to insert elastic into casing

B

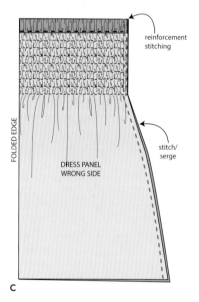

reinforcement
stitching

FOLDED EDGE

DRESS PANEL
WRONG SIDE

stitch/
serge

C

5. Insert the ½˝ knit elastic into the casing from Step 2. Use a bodkin or large safety pin to help guide the elastic through. Secure both ends by stitching close to the edge of the casing. **Fig. B**

6. Fold the dress in half vertically, right sides together, and pin. Pinning is key to ensuring that the shirred rows and the top and bottom edges are perfectly aligned. Stitch/serge from top to bottom. Within the seam allowance, make another row of stitching across all the shirred rows to reinforce this area. Finally, press the seam to the side and topstitch it down to avoid extra bulk, especially where the elastic and elastic threads meet. **Fig. C**

7. See Add-Ons (page 131) to add the straps and ruffled hem if you'd like to finish the dress as photographed.

8. Hem the dress. For woven fabrics, press ¼˝ toward the wrong side and then another ½˝. Topstitch close to the inner folded edge. For knits, create a ¾˝ hem by serging the raw edge, pressing the hem up ¾˝, and stitching close to the edge with a stretch or zigzag stitch. If you use a coverstitch machine to hem, you won't need to serge the edge first. You can also make a lettuce-edge rolled hem on your serger. Refer to Hemming Techniques (page 46).

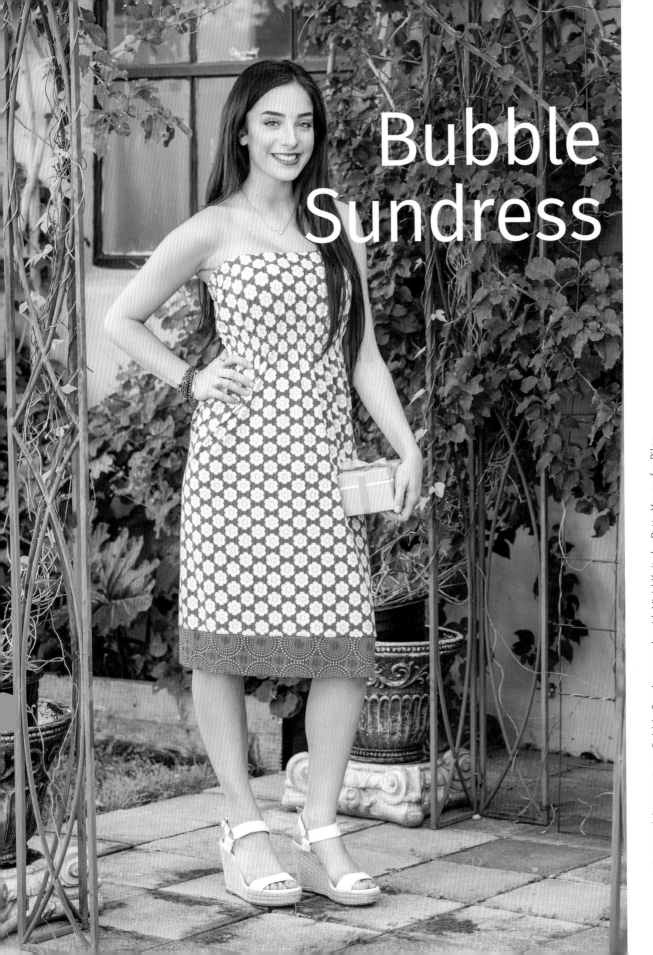

Bubble Sundress

Our model is wearing a Bubble Sundress made with Vivid Knits by Patty Young for Riley Blake Designs. It features a double-layer hem band in a coordinating knit. For hem band instructions, refer to Add-Ons, Straight Double-Layer Hem Band (page 141).

This fun variation on the Simple Sundress is even faster to sew because it has fewer rows of shirring! An unshirred section at the bust makes this dress perfect for sensitive skin.

For instructions, refer to Simple Sundress, Fabric and Notions (page 20).

- ½–1½ yards (depending on size) of ½"-wide knit elastic
- 1 spool of elastic thread
- Coordinating thread
- Rotary cutter and self-healing mat, or dressmaking shears
- Flexible measuring tape

CUTTING

For instructions, refer to Simple Sundress, Cutting (page 20).

Assemble

All seams are ½".

1. Refer to Simple Sundress, Assemble, Steps 1 and 2 (page 21), to create an elastic casing at the top of your dress.

2. For the "bubble" effect, there will be 3 rows of shirring at the top of the dress (directly under the casing) and 4 or 5 rows of shirring under your bust, with the in-between section left to "bubble out." Using a flexible tape

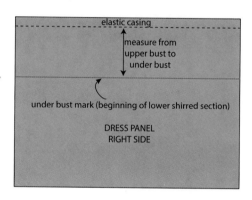

measure, measure from your upper bust to your underbust and transfer this measurement to the fabric. Use a water-soluble marker, some masking tape, or a row of pins (ballpoint for knits) to mark the start of the lower shirred portion on the right side of the fabric.

3. Follow the shirring instructions in Shirr Magic (page 16), working with the dress panel right side up on the sewing machine so the elastic thread will be on the wrong side of your garment, to shirr the upper bust and underbust sections.

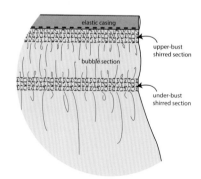

4. Follow Simple Sundress, Assemble, Steps 5–7 (page 22), to insert elastic in the casing, finish the vertical seam, and hem the dress.

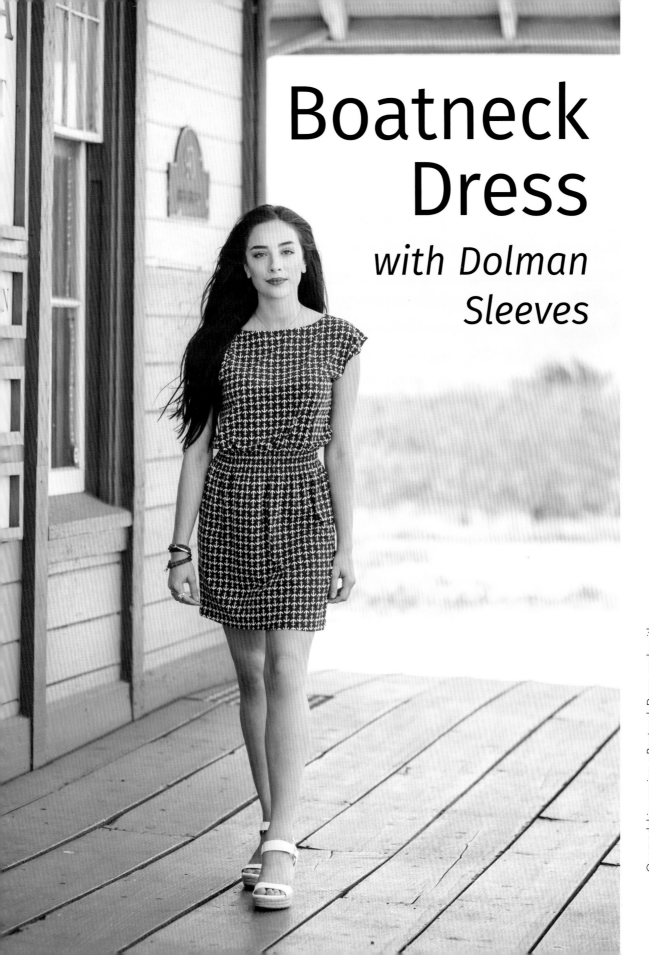

Boatneck
Dress

with Dolman
Sleeves

Classic and fashionable, this dress is perfect for just about any occasion. And since it uses only two cuts of fabric, it sews up in a snap.

FABRIC AND NOTIONS

Use stretch fabrics only, such as cotton interlock, jerseys, rib knits, stretch velvet, or stretch velour, 58″/60″ wide. Avoid thicker fabrics, such as double knits, because they will be difficult to shirr. Refer to Know Your Fabrics (page 7).

The amount of fabric you need to buy will vary depending on size, dress length, and add-ons. Refer to the cutting instructions to determine the yardage. Always purchase at least ¼ yard extra to allow for fabric shrinkage.

- 1 spool of elastic thread
- Coordinating thread
- Rotary cutter and self-healing mat, or dressmaking shears
- Flexible measuring tape
- Optional: Seam tape or clear elastic for stabilizing shoulder seams

CUTTING

These directions are based on fabrics at least 58″ wide. Calculate the width of your dress based on your Hip measurement (E). Base the length on your Dress Length (L).

Cut 2 dress panels following these formulas to get the size. Remember that the maximum stretch of the fabric should go from side to side across the width of your dress panels.

WIDTH: Hips ÷ 2, and then add 3″ for seam allowances and ease. For example, if my Hips measure 40″, the width of each panel will be 40″ ÷ 2 = 20″ + 3″ = 23″.

LENGTH: Dress Length measurement + 1½″ for hem and seam allowances. For example, if my Dress Length (L) measurement is 40″, the length of each panel will be 41½″.

NOTE

For Women/Teens, if your Full Bust measurement is larger than your Hip measurement, use the larger measurement to calculate fabric width.

Fabric Width = Hips ÷ 2 + 3″

Fabric Length = Dress Length + 1½″

FRONT/BACK PANELS

Assemble

All seams are ½".

1. To create the boatneck opening, fold a dress panel in half through the width of the panel as shown, aligning all raw edges and creating a center crease along the length. On the top edge of the fabric, and starting on the center fold, measure 3″ toward the side edge for Girls' sizes 2–5, 4″ for Girls' sizes 6–10, or 5″ for Women's/Teens' sizes. (Measure over further if you'd like a wider boatneck.) Place a pin at that mark. Measure 2″ down from the top edge, along the fold, and place another pin there. With a water-soluble marker, draw a gentle curve from pin to pin, creating the boatneck opening.

2. Along the raw side edges, measure 1″ down from the top and place another pin there. Draw a diagonal line from the outer neck pin to the side pin to create the angled shoulder seams. Cut along both lines and discard the excess fabric. **Fig. A**

3. Repeat Steps 1 and 2 for the second dress panel.

4. Open both dress panels and place them right sides together, aligning all raw edges. Stitch along both shoulder seams, and finish these seams with a serger or zigzag stitch. If you wish, stitch a strip of seam tape or clear elastic within the seam allowance to stabilize the shoulders. **Fig. B**

5. Finish the raw edge of the boatneck opening with a serger or zigzag stitch, and then press the edge ½″ toward the wrong side. Stitch the neck edge down from the right side, using a coverstitch machine, a twin needle, or a wide zigzag stitch.

boat neck width

2″   1″

FOLD

DRESS PANEL WRONG SIDE

SIDE RAW EDGES

A

stitch   stitch

SIDE RAW EDGES   SIDE RAW EDGES

DRESS PANEL WRONG SIDE

B

Bodice Length - 1″

Shirring Positioning Mark

DRESS PANEL
RIGHT SIDE

C

6. Determine where the shirred portion will be positioned: Place the dress panels right side up on your work surface, with side edges and shoulder seams aligned. Subtract 1″ from your Bodice Length (K). Using this new measurement, measure down from the top of the shoulder (outer edge of the boat neck) and place a pin horizontally at your mark. Repeat for the other side of the shoulder and the back dress panel, ending up with 4 horizontal pins. Double-check that your marks are straight and aligned with each other. Using a water-soluble fabric marker, draw a horizontal line across the dress from pin to pin on each panel. This mark will be the start of your shirring. Do not begin to shirr yet! You will close up 1 side of the dress first and leave the other side open for shirring. **Fig.C**

7. Finish the raw edges along both sides of the dress, front and back. From both outer shoulder seams on each panel, measure 5″ down for Girls' sizes 2–5, 7″ down for Girls' sizes 6–10, and 10″ down for Women's/Teens' sizes to mark the arm openings. Place a pin at both sides.

> **NOTE**
>
> *Plus-size women may need a larger arm opening. Use a tape measure and adjust the opening as needed to ensure a perfect fit.*

Place the dress panels right sides together, aligning all outer edges and the front and back shirring lines. Stitch 1 side closed from the armhole pin down to the hem. Backstitch a couple of times at the beginning to reinforce your stitches. Press the seam open. Leave the other side open so you can shirr the waist while the dress is flat.

8. Press the edges above the pin ½˝ to the wrong side and topstitch from the right side of the dress, creating the dolman sleeves. Stitch a straight line where the seams meet at the bottom of the sleeve opening. **Fig.D**

9. Refer to Shirr Magic (page 16) to shirr the waist, working with the dress right side up on the sewing machine so the elastic thread will be on the wrong side of your garment. Start the first row at the line you marked in Step 5. Your machine's needle should enter right on the edge of the mark. Stitch 6 lines of shirring for Girls/Tweens and 8 lines for Women/Teens. When you've finished shirring, backstitch a couple of times to secure the elastic thread.

10. Close up the other side of the dress just as you did in Steps 7 and 8, making sure the shirring rows are aligned at the side. Press the seam to the side and topstitch over the shirring rows to reinforce. **Fig.E**

11. Hem the dress. Create a ¾˝ hem by serging the raw edge, pressing the hem up ¾˝, and stitching close to the edge with a stretch or zigzag stitch. If you use a coverstitch machine to hem, you won't need to serge the edge first. You can also make a lettuce-edge rolled hem on your serger. Refer to Hemming Techniques (page 46).

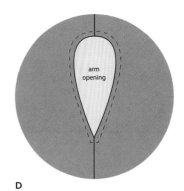

arm opening

D

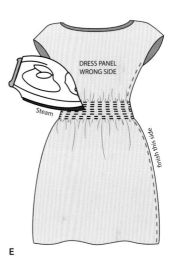

DRESS PANEL
WRONG SIDE

Steam

finish this side

E

VARIATION: *Spice up your Boatneck Dress by adding hem ruffles or patch pockets. Get ideas for all of these items in Add-Ons (page 131).*

Shirred Blouse

with Cap Sleeves

This blouse features a wide shirred panel at the chest and adorable cap sleeves that cover your shoulders.

FABRIC AND NOTIONS

Use stretch fabrics, such as cotton interlock, jerseys, rib knits, stretch velvet, or stretch velour, 58″/60″ wide. Avoid thicker fabrics, such as double knits, because they will be difficult to shirr. Top-weight woven fabrics, such as quilting cottons, shirtings, lawns, voiles, satins, and eyelets, also work well for this style of blouse. Refer to Know Your Fabrics (page 7).

The amount of fabric you need to buy will vary depending on size, blouse length, and add-ons. Refer to the cutting instructions to determine the yardage. Always purchase ¼ yard extra to allow for fabric shrinkage.

- ½–1½ yards (depending on size) of ½″-wide knit elastic
- 1 spool of elastic thread
- Coordinating thread
- Rotary cutter and self-healing mat, or dressmaking shears
- Flexible measuring tape

CUTTING

These directions are based on fabrics at least 58″ wide. Calculate the width of your blouse based on the measurement for C, Chest (Girls/Tweens) or Full Bust (Women/Teens). Base the length on your Strapless Blouse Length (O). Refer to the cutting diagram (page 32). Grab your calculator because you will need it for this one!

1. Cut 1 or 2 blouse panels, depending on the width of your fabric, following these formulas to get the size:

WIDTH: C + ⅓ of C. Round up your numbers. For example, if my Full Bust measures 32″, the width of my fabric will be 32″ + 11″ = 43″.

> **NOTE**
>
> *If the total width of your blouse is wider than the width of your fabric (most knits come in 58″/60″ width and wovens are generally 44″/45″ wide), divide your total width in half, add 1″ for seam allowances, and cut 2 identical pieces.*

LENGTH: Strapless Blouse Length measurement (O) + 1½″. For example, if my Strapless Blouse Length measurement is 16″, the length of my fabric will be 17½″.

If you are busty, you may need extra length in the bodice, to allow for the fitted bust of this top. Measure from the upper bust, holding the flexible measuring tape tight to your body, over the fullest part of your bust, to your underbust, and then straight down to where you would like your top to end.

2. Cut 2 cap sleeve panels:

WIDTH: 4″ for Girls/Tweens or 6″ for Women/Teens

LENGTH: To achieve a perfect fit for the cap sleeves, measure from your upper chest, up over the shoulders, and down to the bottom of your shoulder blade (where your blouse panel will hit) and add 3″ to allow for shirring. Or use the average measurements provided (at right).

GIRLS' SIZES 2–5:
7″ + 3″ (shirring) = 10″ total

GIRLS' SIZES 5–10:
9″ + 3″ (shirring) = 12″ total

TWEENS'/TEENS' SIZES 12–16:
12″ + 3″ (shirring) = 15″ total

WOMEN'S/TEENS' SIZES 2–10:
14″ + 3″ shirring = 17″ total

WOMEN'S/TEENS' SIZES 12–16:
15″ + 3″ (shirring) = 18″ total

WOMEN'S/TEENS' SIZES 18 AND UP:
16″ + 3″ (shirring) = 19″ total

3. Cut the ½″-wide elastic:

LENGTH:

GIRLS' SIZES: C – 2″

WOMEN'S/TEENS' SIZES: Upper Bust (B) – 2″

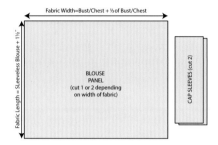

Fabric Width=Bust/Chest + ⅓ of Bust/Chest

Fabric Length = Sleeveless Blouse + 1½″

BLOUSE PANEL (cut 1 or 2 depending on width of fabric)

CAP SLEEVES (cut 2)

Assemble

All seams are ½″.

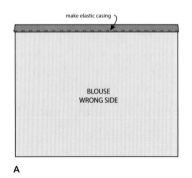

make elastic casing

BLOUSE WRONG SIDE

A

NOTE

If you use a coverstitch machine, you don't need to serge or zigzag first. Just stitch the raw edge down after pressing.

1. If you cut 2 panels for your blouse, the seams will be on the sides. Place the fabric right sides together with the side seams aligned and stitch down 1 side only. Finish the seam with a serger or a zigzag stitch and press to the side. Leave the other side open so you can shirr the garment while it is still flat.

If your blouse will be made from a single panel, the seam will be in the back. No need to sew up any seams at this point; you will want to shirr the garment while the fabric is flat. **Fig. A**

2. Serge or finish the top edge of the blouse panel with a zigzag stitch. Create an elastic casing at the top of the blouse panel by folding the top edge down ¾″ toward the wrong side, pressing well, and then stitching over the serged/finished edge from side to side of the blouse. Don't insert the elastic yet. It's much easier to do this after you shirr the top portion of the blouse.

3. Hem the 2 long edges of both cap sleeves with a narrow hem (no more than ¼″ wide) or a rolled hem. Set aside. **Fig. B**

B

4. Determine the width of the portion to be shirred by measuring from the upper bust down to the underbust for Women/Teens, or from the armpit down to where you want the shirring to end for Girls/Tweens. Typically, you want the shirring to cover just the chest area to create an empire waist. Round up to the next multiple of ¼″ if your measurement is between quarter marks. Measure down this amount from the top folded edge of your fabric to mark where the shirring should end on the right side of the fabric, using a water-soluble fabric marker, masking tape, or a row of pins (ballpoint for knits). **Fig. C**

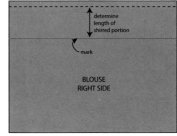

C

5. Follow the shirring instructions in Shirr Magic (page 16) to stitch the shirring rows on the bodice, working with the blouse panel right side up on the sewing machine so the elastic thread will be on the wrong side. Make sure the rows of shirring are the exact width of your standard presser foot and the last row aligns with your mark. Shoot the section with steam to gather the fabric fully. **Fig. D**

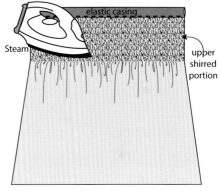

D

6. To shirr the cap sleeves, place a cap sleeve piece right side up with the edge of your sewing machine's presser foot against the hemmed edge. This will determine where to place the first row of shirring. Stitch 6 rows of vertical shirring on each sleeve, 3 on each side with a center section that will "bubble" out. Shoot the sleeves with a bit of steam to make sure the shirring is fully gathered. **Fig. E**

E

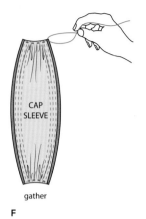

gather

F

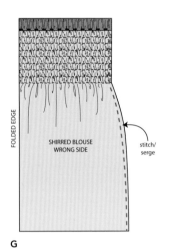

FOLDED EDGE

SHIRRED BLOUSE
WRONG SIDE

stitch/
serge

G

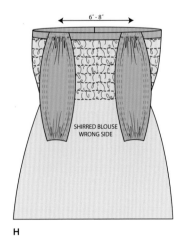

6˝ - 8˝

SHIRRED BLOUSE
WRONG SIDE

H

7. Gather the raw ends of the sleeves by stitching close to the short raw edge of each sleeve with your longest machine stitch and then pulling the bobbin thread to gather each sleeve to half its original width. This will create the cap sleeve effect. Finish the gathered edge with a serger or zigzag stitch. Set the sleeves aside. **Fig. F**

8. Insert the ½˝ knit elastic into the casing at the top of the blouse panel. Use a bodkin or large safety pin to help guide the elastic through. Secure both ends by stitching close to the edge of the casing.

9. Fold the blouse in half, right sides together, and stitch/serge from top to bottom. Pinning is key to ensuring that the shirred rows and top and bottom edges are perfectly aligned. Within the seam allowance, make another row of stitching across all the shirred rows to reinforce this area. Finally, press the seam to the side and topstitch it down to avoid extra bulk, especially where the elastic and elastic threads meet. **Fig. G**

10. Place the finished blouse wrong side out on a flat surface with the elasticized end at the top. If you've constructed the blouse from 2 pieces of fabric, the seams should be at the sides. If you've constructed the blouse with a single piece of fabric, perfectly center the seam at the back.

Mark the center front and back of the blouse, and then measure 3˝ to the left and right of the center mark for Girls/Tweens or 4˝ to the left and right for Women/Teens. This is your sleeve positioning mark.

11. Center a cap sleeve over a sleeve positioning mark, *right side facing up*, with the gathered edge aligned with the edge of the elastic casing. Pin, and then stitch ½˝ down from the casing edge. Repeat this step with the other cap sleeve. **Fig. H**

12. Wrap both sleeves toward the back of the blouse *under the bottom*, and pin both gathered ends to the top edge of the bodice back in the same manner as the front. The sleeves will be shorter than the blouse, so it will be scrunched up between the sleeves at this point. Stitch ½˝ from the edge. **Fig.I**

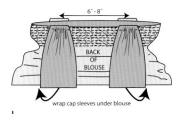

wrap cap sleeves under blouse

I

13. Turn the blouse and sleeves right side out so the sleeves are above the shirred bodice. Topstitch the sleeves down ⅛˝ from the top edge of the blouse, as shown. **Fig.J**

14. Hem the blouse. For woven fabrics, press ¼˝ toward the wrong side and then another ½˝. Topstitch close to the inner folded edge. For knits, create a ¾˝ hem by serging the raw edge, pressing the hem up ¾˝, and stitching close to the edge with a stretch or zigzag stitch. If you use a coverstitch machine to hem, you won't need to serge the edge first. You can also make a lettuce-edge rolled hem on your serger. Refer to Hemming Techniques (page 46).

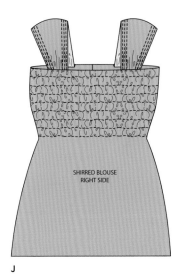

SHIRRED BLOUSE
RIGHT SIDE

J

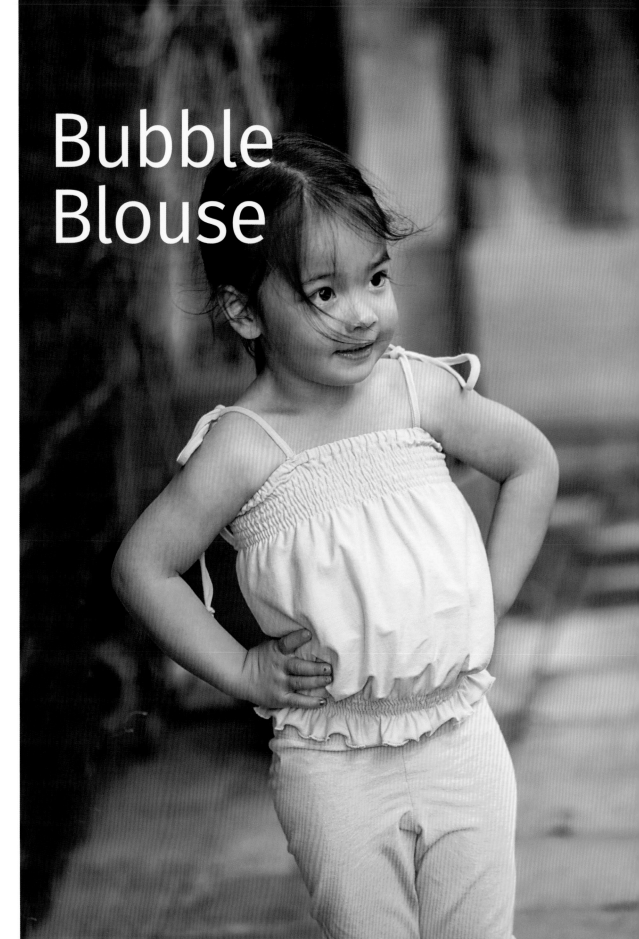

Bubble Blouse

Our model is wearing a Bubble Blouse made with Solid Aqua Jersey Knit by Riley Blake Designs.

This comfortable blouse has shirring at the chest and waist with the middle portion left to bubble out. A couple of optional spaghetti straps keep the top in place while adding a bit of extra flair. It looks adorable on kids and women alike. Learn how to sew the spaghetti straps in Add-Ons, Spaghetti Straps (page 138).

FABRIC AND NOTIONS

Use stretch fabrics, such as cotton interlock, jerseys, rib knits, stretch velvet, or stretch velour, 58″/60″ wide. Avoid thicker fabrics, such as double knits, because they will be difficult to shirr. Top-weight woven fabrics, such as quilting cottons, shirtings, lawns, voiles, satins, and eyelets, also work well for this style of blouse. Refer to Know Your Fabrics (page 7).

The amount of fabric you need to buy will vary depending on size, blouse length, and add-ons. Refer to the cutting instructions to determine the yardage. Always purchase ¼ yard extra to allow for fabric shrinkage.

- 1–2 yards (depending on size) of ½″-wide knit elastic

- 1 spool of elastic thread

- Coordinating thread

- Rotary cutter and self-healing mat, or dressmaking shears

- Flexible measuring tape

CUTTING

These directions are based on fabrics at least 58″ wide.

1. To cut the bodice panel(s) and elastic, refer to the instructions for Shirred Blouse, Cutting (page 31).

2. To cut the straps, refer to the instructions for Add-Ons, Spaghetti Straps (page 138).

NOTE

If the total width of your blouse is wider than the width of your fabric (most knits are 58″/60″ wide, and wovens are generally 44″/45″ wide), divide the total width in half, add 1″ for seam allowances, and cut 2 identical pieces.

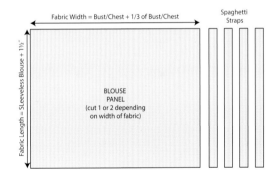

Assemble

All seams are ½˝.

1. Follow Shirred Blouse, Assemble, Steps 1 and 2 (page 32), to sew a side seam, if needed, and make the casing on the bodice.

2. Repeat Shirred Blouse, Assemble, Step 4 (page 33), to mark the upper shirring.

3. Measure 3˝ up from the bottom raw edge of your blouse panel and mark the upper edge of the lower shirring, as you did in the previous step. **Fig. A**

4. Follow the shirring instructions in Shirr Magic (page 16) to shirr the upper and lower sections of the blouse, working with the blouse panel right side up on the sewing machine so the elastic thread will be on the wrong side. For the "bubble" effect, you should stitch 3 or 4 rows of shirring at the bottom of the blouse, just above the hem, with the in-between section left to "bubble out." Make sure the rows of shirring in each section are the width of your standard presser foot. Shoot the shirred sections with steam to gather the fabric fully. **Fig. B**

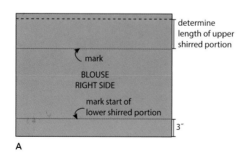

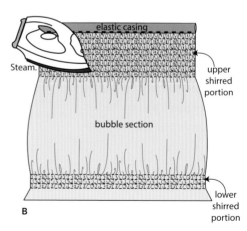

5. Insert the ½˝ knit elastic into the casing at the upper edge of the bodice. Use a bodkin or large safety pin to help guide the elastic through. Secure both ends by stitching close to the edge of the casing.

6. Close up the blouse by folding it in half, right sides together, and pinning along the raw edges. Pinning is key to making sure all the shirring rows and the top and bottom edges are perfectly aligned. Stitch/serge from top to bottom along the open edges. Run another row of stitching across all the shirred rows within the seam allowance to reinforce this area. Finally, press the seam to the side and topstitch it down to avoid extra bulk, especially where the elastic and elastic threads meet. **Fig. C**

7. Make and attach the straps, following the directions for Add-Ons, Spaghetti Straps (page 138).

Try the blouse on and tie the front and back straps into a bow at the shoulders where comfortable.

8. Hem the blouse. For woven fabrics, press ¼˝ toward the wrong side and then another ½˝. Topstitch close to the inner folded edge. For knits, create a ¾˝ hem by serging the raw edge, pressing the hem up ¾˝, and stitching close to the edge with a stretch or zigzag stitch. If you use a coverstitch machine to hem, you won't need to serge the edge first. You can also make a lettuce-edge rolled hem on your serger. Refer to Hemming Techniques (page 46).

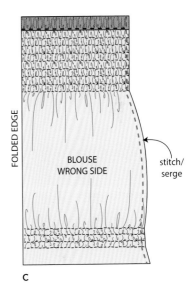

FOLDED EDGE

BLOUSE WRONG SIDE

stitch/ serge

C

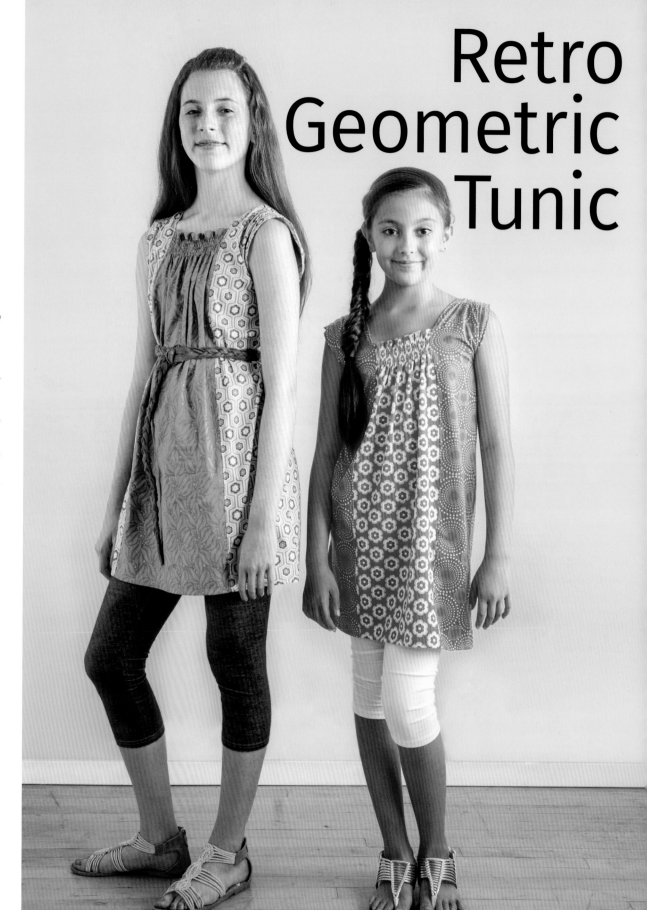

Retro Geometric Tunic

This 70s throwback A-line tunic or dress is oh, so chic, and perfect for all your solid fabrics or funky geometric prints. The tunic is made from six panels, three in the front and three in the back. The middle front and back panels are shorter at the top and much wider than the side panels. Shirring at the shoulders and top center panels creates the A-line silhouette.

Shirring at shoulders and center gore

FABRIC AND NOTIONS

Use stretch fabrics, such as cotton interlock, jerseys, rib knits, stretch velvet, or stretch velour, 58″/60″ wide. Avoid thicker fabrics, such as double knits, because they will be difficult to shirr. Top-weight woven fabrics, such as quilting cottons, shirtings, lawns, voiles, satins, and eyelets, also work well for this style of dress. Refer to Know Your Fabrics (page 7).

The amount of fabric you need to buy will vary depending on size, dress or tunic length, and add-ons. Refer to the cutting instructions to determine the yardage. Always purchase ¼ yard extra to allow for fabric shrinkage.

- 1 spool of elastic thread
- Coordinating thread
- Rotary cutter and self-healing mat, or dressmaking shears
- Flexible measuring tape

CUTTING

These directions are based on fabrics at least 58″ wide. Calculate the width of your dress based on your Hip measurement (E). Base the length of the side panels on your Dress Length (L) and of the middle panels on your Strapless Dress Length (M). Grab your calculator because you will need it for this one!

1. Cut 4 side panels following this formula to get the size:

WIDTH: Hip measurement ÷ 6, round up to the nearest whole number, and then add 1″ for seam allowances. For example, if my Hips measure 40″, my panel width will be 40″ ÷ 6 = 7″ (rounded up) + 1″ = 8″.

LENGTH: Dress Length measurement + 1¼″ for seam and hem allowances, or shorter if you want it more like tunic length

Label them "front right," "front left," "back right," and "back left."

2. Cut 2 middle panels following this formula to get the size:

WIDTH: Hip measurement ÷ 6, and then add 7″ to allow for ease (see Tip, page 42). For example, if my Hips measure 40″, my middle panel width will be 40″ ÷ 6 = 7″ (rounded up) + 7″ = 14″.

LENGTH: Strapless Dress Length measurement + 1½″ for top and bottom hem allowances, or the same amount shorter if you changed the length of the side panels

Label them "front middle" and "back middle."

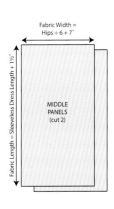

Assemble

All seams are ½". "Right" and "left" refer to reader's point of view.

1. Make a traditional ¾" double-fold hem on what will be the upper end of the front and back middle panels by folding the raw edge ¼" toward the wrong side, then another ½", and stitching close to the inner folded edge. Set the middle panels aside.

2. Place the front right and back right panels right sides together, aligning all edges. Pin and then stitch across 1 short edge only to create a shoulder seam. Finish this seam with a serger or zigzag stitch. Repeat this step with the front left and back left panels.

3. Open the side panels flat. Following the shirring instructions in Shirr Magic (page 16), place the presser foot against the shoulder seam and stitch 3 lines of shirring parallel to the shoulder seam, in both the front and back panels. **Fig. A**

4. On both the front and back middle panels, stitch 6 lines of shirring parallel to the top hemmed edge. **Fig. B**

5. Shoot all shirred areas with a bit of steam to gather them as much as possible.

> **TIP**
>
> *"Ease" refers to the space between the garment and your body. Without added ease, your dress or tunic won't have an A-line silhouette and will fit tightly on your body. If you prefer a looser fit, add more ease in the middle panels, and if you prefer a tighter fit, reduce the ease. Add extra ease in the middle panels only, not the side panels.*

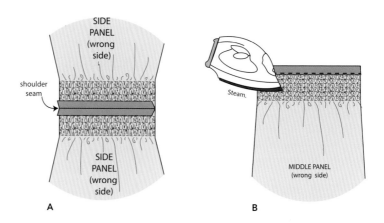

A

B

6. Place the front middle panel on top of the front left side panel, right sides together and the raw edges aligned at the bottom and sides. Make sure the side panel is opened up at the shoulder seam so it's only a single layer. Pin the side and middle panel together from the bottom edge to the top hemmed edge of the middle panel, leaving the side panel extending above the middle panel. Stitch together, backstitching at the top of the hemmed edge to reinforce. **Fig. C**

7. Repeat Step 6 to attach the front right side panel to the other long edge of the front middle panel, and then sew the back middle panel to the inner edges of the back left and right side panels, ending with a tunic joined at the shoulders but open on the outer sides. **Fig. D**

8. Finish all the seams stitched in Steps 6 and 7, as well as the unstitched edges above the middle panel, using a serger or zigzag stitch. Press all the seams and the serged edges toward the side panels. Topstitch the side panels from the front bottom edge all the way to the back bottom edge, hemming the inner neckline areas in the process. **Fig. E**

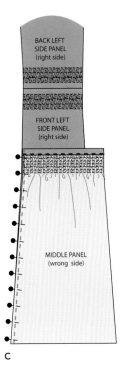

C

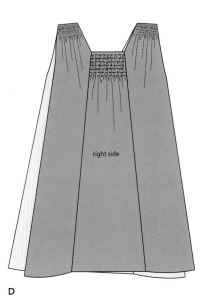

D

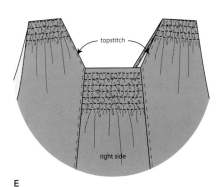

E

9. Using a serger or a zigzag stitch on your sewing machine, finish the raw edges of the sides.

10. Turn the garment inside out and align the outer side and bottom edges.

11. From the shoulder seam, measure down the outer side edges 5˝ for Girls' sizes 2–5, 7˝ for Girls' sizes 6–10, and 10˝ for Women's/Teens' sizes. Place a pin at both sides. This will be your arm opening.

Stitch the sides closed, starting at the pin and stitching down to the hem. Make sure you backstitch a couple of times at the beginning to reinforce your stitches. Press the side seams open.

12. Press the edges above the pin ½˝ to the wrong side and topstitch from the right side of the dress, creating the sleeve opening. Stitch a straight line across where the seams meet at the bottom of the sleeve opening. Fig.F

13. Hem the tunic. For woven fabrics, press ¼˝ toward the wrong side and then another ½˝. Topstitch close to the inner folded edge. For knits, create a ¾˝ hem by serging the raw edge, pressing the hem up ¾˝, and stitching close to the edge with a stretch or zigzag stitch. If you use a coverstitch machine to hem, you won't need to serge the edge first. You can also make a lettuce-edge rolled hem on your serger. Refer to Hemming Techniques (page 46).

NOTE

Plus-size women may need a larger arm opening. Use a tape measure and adjust the opening as needed to ensure a perfect fit.

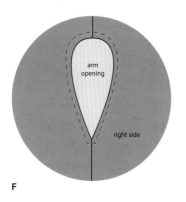

F

Stretch Yourself

The projects in this chapter are made either with stretchy fabric, such as knits, or with stretchy waistbands. You will learn how to create three different types of waistbands: a yoga band, a flat-fronted waistband with back elastic casing, and a soft-elastic waistband. Once you learn how to create all these, you will be able to use them in many applications to create your own custom garments.

Refer to Know Your Fabrics (page 7) for more information on how to determine the correct amount of stretch your fabric should have for each project.

You will learn how to create three different types of waistbands

Hemming Techniques

Check out the myriad of hemming options for knit garments, from the most professional to the easiest.

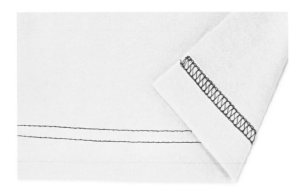

Coverstitch hem

Rolled hem

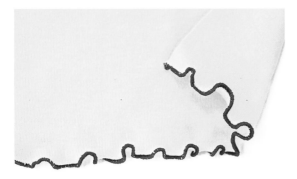

Lettuce-edge hem

COVERSTITCH   This is the twin- or triple-needle stitching you see on the hems of most ready-to-wear knit garments. The top looks like parallel rows of straight stitching and the underside looks like serger loops that cover the raw edge. To make this stitch, you will need a coverstitch machine or a serger with a cover-stitch function.

ROLLED HEM   A narrow, dense stitch made on the edge of the fabric. If you own a serger, a rolled hem is a quick and easy way to finish a knit garment and a great way to add pizazz by using a contrasting thread color. Make sure you use a textured thread, such as Woolly Nylon, Polyarn, or Bulky Nylon, on the upper looper to get that thick, rich-looking rolled hem. Follow your serger's instructions for a three-thread rolled hem.

LETTUCE EDGE   To give the edge of your garment a wavy, ruffled finish like lettuce leaves, make a rolled hem but set your serger's differential feed to maximum stretch and also stretch the fabric slightly with your fingers while you feed it through.

FAUX COVERSTITCH Fool even the most discerning eye into thinking you finished your garment with a coverstitch machine by using a stretch twin needle on your sewing machine. To achieve this look, press the hem toward the wrong side. Using a medium stitch length and a stretch twin needle, stitch the hem down from the right side of the garment. Use a textured thread, such as Woolly Nylon, Polyarn, or Bulky Nylon, in the bobbin to give your hems maximum elasticity.

ZIGZAG STITCH For a funky, homemade look, press the hem toward the wrong side. Set your sewing machine to a zigzag stitch at medium stitch length and stitch the hem down from the right side of the garment. Use a textured thread, such as Woolly Nylon, Polyarn, or Bulky Nylon, in the bobbin to give your hem maximum elasticity.

RAW EDGE For a more shabby-chic or grungy look, leave the hem unfinished on knits. Knit fabrics will not ravel, but the raw edges might curl up a bit over time.

Faux coverstitch hem

Zigzag hem

A-Line Skirt

Casual and comfortable, this A-Line Skirt looks fabulous with all your favorite tops and can be layered over leggings or tights for the cooler months.

FABRIC AND NOTIONS

Use knit fabrics only, such as cotton interlock, jerseys, rib knits, stretch velvet, or stretch velour, 58″/60″ wide. Avoid thicker fabrics, such as double knits. Make sure your knit skirt fabric has at least 25% stretch. Refer to the stretch gauge diagram (page 9) in Know Your Fabrics. For the yoga waistband, your fabric must contain at least 4% Lycra (spandex).

The amount of fabric you need to buy will vary depending on size and skirt length. Refer to the cutting instructions to determine the yardage. Always purchase ¼ yard extra to allow for fabric shrinkage.

- Coordinating thread
- Rotary cutter and self-healing mat, or dressmaking shears
- Flexible measuring tape
- Water-soluble fabric marker

CUTTING

These directions are based on fabrics at least 58″ wide. Calculate the skirt width based on your Hip measurement (E). Base the length on your Skirt Length measurement (N).

1. Cut 2 skirt panels following these formulas to get the size:

WIDTH: Hip measurement ÷ 2, and then add 8″. For example, if my Hips (E) measure 40″, the width of my panels will be 40″ ÷ 2 = 20″ + 8″ = 28″.

LENGTH: Skirt Length measurement, no extra length

2. Cut 2 waistband panels:

WIDTH: Waist measurement ÷ 2, and then subtract 1″. For example, if my Waist measures 30″, the width of each waistband panel will be 30″ ÷ 2 = 15″ – 1″ = 14″.

HEIGHT: 9″, regardless of size

NOTE

Remember that the maximum stretch of the skirt and waistband fabric should always go from side to side—across the width of these panels, not the height/length.

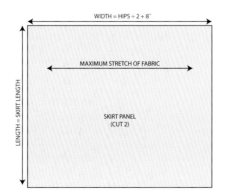

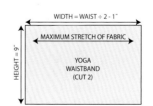

Assemble

All seams are ½".

1. Place the skirt panels right sides together on a flat surface, aligning all raw edges. Determine which end will be the skirt top and place a pin at the center point.

2. Divide your Waist measurement (D) by 4. For example, if my Waist measures 30", then 30" ÷ 4 = 7½". Place a pin at this measurement to the left and right of the center mark.

3. Using a water-soluble fabric marker, draw a diagonal line from the left bottom raw-edge corner of the skirt panel to the left pin and from the right bottom corner to the right pin. **Fig. A**

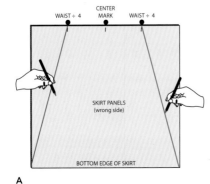

A

4. Using a rotary cutter, ruler, and self-healing mat, cut along the lines you drew in Step 3, creating 2 A-line skirt panels. Discard the excess fabric or save for a future project (these smallish pieces would work for pockets or skinny straps).

5. With the fabric panels still right sides together, stitch/serge along both angled sides. **Fig. B**

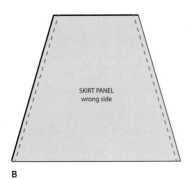

B

6. Finish the bottom raw edge of the skirt with a serger or zigzag stitch, and then press the edge up ¾". Hem the skirt using your preferred hemming method. See Hemming Techniques (page 46).

7. To create the yoga waistband, place the waistband panels right sides together, with all raw edges perfectly aligned. Stitch/serge together along the 9" edges to make a loop.

8. Fold the waistband in half, wrong sides together, encasing both side seams, and press the fold at the top to create a nice crease. **Fig. C**

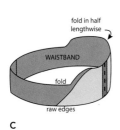

C

9. To attach the waistband to the finished skirt, lay the waistband over the right side of the skirt's top edge, aligning side seams and keeping raw edges even.

> **NOTE**
>
> *The waistband will be narrower than the top edge of the skirt. Pin first in quarters and then all around, stretching the waistband's raw edges slightly to fit.*

Stitch/serge ½˝ from raw edges. Turn the waistband right side out and press the seam down. **Fig. D**

The waistband can be worn folded all the way down, halfway down, or pulled up.

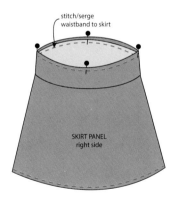

Our adult model's skirt is made with Heaven & Helsinki jersey knit fabric by Patty Young for Michael Miller Fabrics.

Maxi Skirt

Both of our models are wearing Maxi Skirts made with jersey knits from Riley Blake Designs.

A maxi skirt is a wardrobe staple these days. It can be casual for shopping or dressy for a party or other event, depending on which fabrics you use. And since this project is super easy to sew, you can make one for every fun event in your life!

FABRIC AND NOTIONS

Use knit fabrics only, such as cotton interlock, jerseys, rib knits, stretch velvet, or stretch velour, 58″/60″ wide. Avoid thicker fabrics, such as double knits. Make sure your knit fabric has at least 25% stretch. Refer to the stretch gauge diagram (page 9) in Know Your Fabrics. For the yoga waistband, your fabric must contain at least 4% Lycra (spandex).

The amount of fabric you need to buy will vary depending on size, skirt length, and add-ons. Refer to the cutting instructions to determine the yardage. Always purchase ¼ yard extra to allow for fabric shrinkage.

- Coordinating thread
- Rotary cutter and self-healing mat, or dressmaking shears
- Flexible measuring tape
- Water-soluble fabric marker

CUTTING

These directions are based on fabrics at least 58″ wide. Calculate the width of your skirt based on your Hip measurement (E). Base the length of your skirt on your Outseam measurement (J).

1. Cut 2 skirt panels following these formulas to get the size:

WIDTH: Hip measurement ÷ 2, and then add 8″. For example, if my Hips measure 40″, the width of my fabric piece will be 40″ ÷ 2 = 20″ + 8″ = 28″.

LENGTH: Outseam measurement without adding any extra length

2. Cut 2 yoga waistband panels:

WIDTH: Waist measurement ÷ 2, and then subtract 1″. For example, if my Waist measures 30″, the width of each waistband panel will be 30″ ÷ 2 = 15″ − 1″ = 14″.

HEIGHT: 9″ high, regardless of size

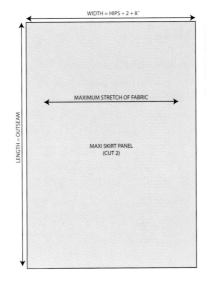

NOTE

Remember that the maximum stretch of the skirt and waistband fabric should always go from side to side—across the width of these panels, not the height/length.

Assemble

To make a skirt without the side slits, follow the directions under A-Line Skirt, Assemble (page 50). To make a skirt with side slits, follow the directions under A-line Skirt, Assemble, but replace Step 5 with the following instructions.

All seams are ½".

1. Place both skirt panels right sides together, aligning all raw edges.

2. Measure from the bottom edge of the skirt panel to just below your knee, or use the following basic measurements:

GIRLS' SIZES 2T–5T: 10"

GIRLS' SIZES 6–10: 12"–14", depending on height

WOMEN'S/TEENS' SIZES: 16"–18", depending on height

Mark the spot on 1 or both sides of the skirt with a pin or water-soluble fabric marker.

3. Stitch the sides of the skirt together, stopping at the side slit marks and backstitching a couple of times. If you want only a single side slit, sew the entire length of the other side. Fig. A

4. Finish the raw edge of each slit separately, using a serger or zigzag stitch.

5. Press the seam above the mark open. Press the edges of the slit ½" toward the wrong side.

6. Topstitch each slit ¼" from the pressed edge, starting at a side of the hem, pivoting at the top of the slit, and ending at the other side. Fig. B

7. Finish the bottom raw edge of the skirt with a serger or zigzag stitch, and then press the edge up ¾". Hem the skirt, using your preferred hemming method. See Hemming Techniques (page 46).

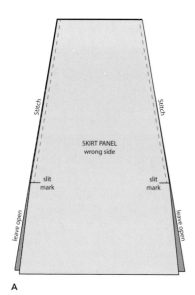

A

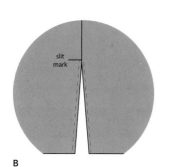

B

High-Low Skirt

Both models are wearing High-Low Skirts made with ruffled knit fabrics from Jo-Ann Fabric and Craft Stores. Our younger model's skirt shows a visible waistband made with wide knit elastic. Our teen model's skirt has a fabric-covered elastic waistband. A lettuce-edge rolled hem is the perfect finishing touch for these skirts.

This skirt features an asymmetrical hemline that is all business in the front and party in the back. Learn how to draft your own pattern for this trendy style and be ready to rock this skirt in one easy afternoon.

FABRIC AND NOTIONS

Use knit fabrics only, such as cotton interlock, jerseys, rib knits, stretch velvet, or stretch velour, 58″/60″ wide. Avoid thicker fabrics, such as double knits. Make sure your knit fabric has at least 25% stretch. Refer to the stretch gauge diagram (page 9) in Know Your Fabrics. If you are using a ruffle knit, like the fabric in our samples, you may want a different fabric or wide knit elastic for the waistband.

The amount of fabric you need to buy will vary depending on size, skirt length, and add-ons. Refer to the cutting instructions to determine the yardage. Always purchase ¼ yard extra to allow for fabric shrinkage.

- ¾″-wide knit or non-roll elastic (enough for your Waist measurement)
- Coordinating thread
- Rotary cutter and self-healing mat, or dressmaking shears
- Flexible measuring tape
- Water-soluble fabric marker

CUTTING

These directions are based on fabrics at least 58″ wide. Calculate the width of your skirt based on your Hip measurement (E). Base the length on your Skirt Length measurement (N).

1. Cut 2 skirt panels following these formulas to get the size:

WIDTH: Hip measurement ÷ 2, and then add 8″. For example, if my Hips measure 40″, the width of my fabric piece will be 40″ ÷ 2 = 20″ + 8″ = 28″.

LENGTH: Skirt Length measurement + 12″

2. Cut 2 waistband panels following this formula to get the size (optional):

WIDTH: Waist measurement ÷ 2. For example, if my Waist measures 30″, the width of each waistband panel will be 30″ ÷ 2 = 15″.

HEIGHT: 3″, regardless of size

> **NOTES**
>
> *You may use wide knit elastic without sewing a casing to attach this visible elastic to your skirt, see Flowy Tulip Skirt, Assemble (page 90).*
>
> *Remember that the maximum stretch of the skirt and waistband fabric should always go from side to side—across the width of these panels, not the height/length.*

3. Cut the ¾″-wide elastic.

WIDTH: Waist measurement (D) – 1″

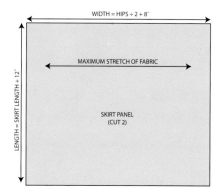

WIDTH = HIPS ÷ 2 + 8″

MAXIMUM STRETCH OF FABRIC

LENGTH = SKIRT LENGTH + 12″

SKIRT PANEL
(CUT 2)

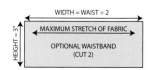

WIDTH = WAIST ÷ 2

MAXIMUM STRETCH OF FABRIC

HEIGHT = 3″

OPTIONAL WAISTBAND
(CUT 2)

Assemble

All seams are ½".

1. Fold each skirt panel widthwise, aligning all raw edges.

2. Divide your Waist measurement by 4. For example, if my Waist measures 30", then 30" ÷ 4 = 7½". Along the top edge of each folded panel, place a pin at ¼ the Waist measurement in from the fold.

3. Place another pin 6" up from the bottom outer side corner of each panel, as shown.

4. Using a water-soluble fabric marker, draw a diagonal line from the top pin to the bottom. **Fig. A**

5. Using a rotary cutter, ruler, and self-healing mat, cut each panel along the diagonal line. Discard the excess fabric or save for a future project. (These smallish pieces would work for pockets or skinny straps!) Do not remove the pins yet.

6. On only 1 skirt panel, place a mark 12" up from the bottom edge along the fold of the fabric. Draw a curved line from the 12" mark on the fold down to the 6" mark on the raw edge, essentially creating a concave curve for your "high" front hemline. Cut along the curved line and discard the excess fabric. **Fig. B**

7. On the remaining panel, draw a convex curve from the bottom folded corner up to the 6" side mark, creating the "low" hem. Cut along this line and discard the excess fabric. **Fig. C**

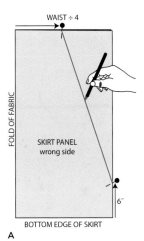

A

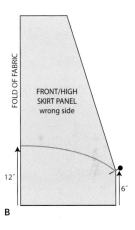

B

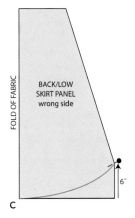

C

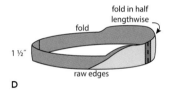

fold in half lengthwise

fold

1 ½″

raw edges

D

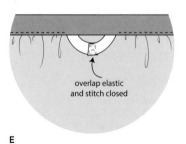

overlap elastic and stitch closed

E

8. Place the panels right sides together, aligning top and side raw edges. Stitch/serge along both diagonal sides.

9. Place the waistband panels right sides together with all raw edges aligned. Stitch/serge along both short edges.

10. Fold the waistband in half, wrong sides together, encasing both side seams, and press the fold at the top to create a nice crease. **Fig. D**

11. To attach the waistband to the finished skirt, place the waistband over the right side of the skirt's top edge, aligning side seams and keeping raw edges even. Pin first in quarters and then all around. Stitch ½″ from raw edges, leaving a 1″ gap in the back for inserting the elastic.

12. Using a large safety pin or a bodkin, insert the elastic inside the gap you left in the waistband in Step 11, and maneuver it all the way around the casing. Pull the other end of the elastic out of the opening, overlapping the ends by ½″, and stitch the ends closed using a box with an X, as shown. **Fig. E**

13. Stitch/serge the gap closed, and press the seam down.

14. Hem the skirt using your preferred hemming method. I love making a lettuce-edge rolled hem with my serger, but a narrow hem also works well for this skirt style.

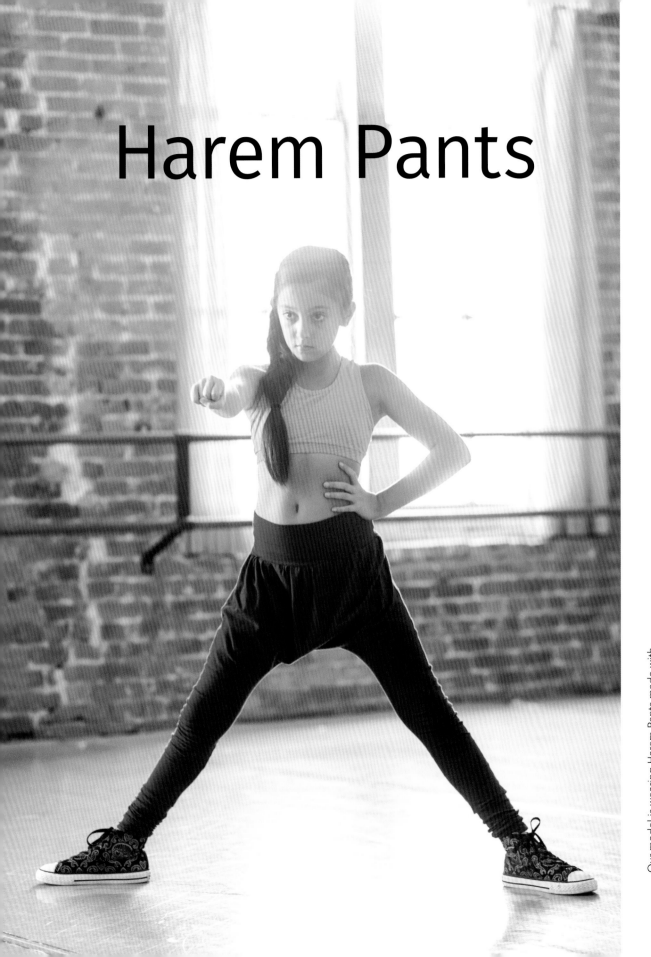

Harem Pants

Our model is wearing Harem Pants made with solid navy jersey knit from Riley Blake Designs.

Whether you are wearing them to take a hip-hop dance class or just to make a fashion statement, these drop-crotch harem pants will be the most comfortable garment you own. With their slouchy silhouette and the no-elastic yoga bands at the waist and ankles, these pants will conform to every body shape.

With yoga waistband and cuffs

FABRIC AND NOTIONS

Use knit fabrics only, such as cotton interlock, jerseys, rib knits, stretch velvet, or stretch velour, 58″/60″ wide. Avoid thicker fabrics, such as double knits. Make sure your knit fabric has at least 25% stretch. Refer to the stretch gauge diagram (page 9) in Know Your Fabrics. For the yoga waistband, your fabric must contain at least 4% Lycra (spandex).

The amount of fabric you need to buy will vary depending on size and pant length. Allow about 1¼–1½ yards for Girls/Tweens and 2–2½ yards for Women/Teens. Don't cut the fabric until you are absolutely sure you have enough! Refer to the cutting information first.

- Coordinating thread
- Rotary cutter and self-healing mat, or dressmaking shears
- Flexible measuring tape
- Water-soluble fabric marker

CUTTING

These directions are based on knit fabrics at least 58″ wide. Calculate the width of your pants based on your Hip measurement (E). Base the length on your Outseam measurement (J).

1. Cut 2 pants panels following these formulas to get the size:

WIDTH: Hip measurement (E) ÷ 2, and then add 8″ for Girls/Tweens or 12″ for Women/Teens. For example, if my Hips measure 40″, the width of my fabric pieces will be 40″ ÷ 2 = 20″ + 12″ = 32″.

LENGTH: Outseam measurement – 2″ to allow for the added length of the waist and ankle bands

2. Cut 2 waistband panels:

WIDTH: Waist measurement (D) ÷ 2, and then subtract 1″. For example, if my Waist measures 30″, the width of each waistband panel will be 30″ ÷ 2 = 15″ – 1″ = 14″.

HEIGHT: 9″ regardless of size

3. Cut 4 ankle cuff panels.

WIDTH: Ankle measurement (F) ÷ 2, and then add 1″

HEIGHT: 5″ regardless of size

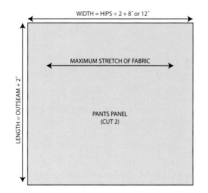

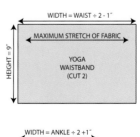

Assemble

All seams are ½".

1. Fold each pants panel in half widthwise as shown, aligning all raw edges and creating a center crease along the length.

Subtract 4"–6" from your Inseam measurement (I), depending on how low you would like the drop crotch to be. Along the folded edge, place a pin at that measurement up from the bottom corner.

> **NOTE**
>
> *Subtract even more if you'd like a more exaggerated drop crotch.*

From the outer bottom corner of the fabric, place a pin at the width of your ankle cuffs + 1". Using a water-soluble marker, draw a curve connecting the 2 pins. Cut along this curve. Layer the cut pants piece over the uncut piece to use as a template, and cut the second panel to the same shape. Discard the excess fabric or save for a future project. (These smallish pieces would work for pockets or skinny straps!) **Fig. A**

2. Place the pant panels right sides together, aligning all raw edges. Stitch/serge both side seams and the drop crotch. **Fig. B**

3. To create the yoga waistband, place the waistband panels right sides together, with all raw edges perfectly aligned. Stitch/serge along the short edges.

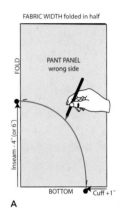

FABRIC WIDTH folded in half

FOLD

PANT PANEL
wrong side

Inseam – 4" (or 6")

BOTTOM   Cuff +1"

A

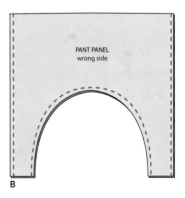

PANT PANEL
wrong side

B

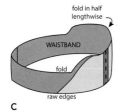

fold in half
lengthwise

WAISTBAND

fold

raw edges

C

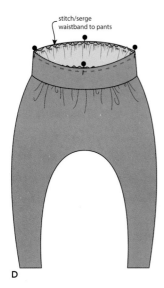

stitch/serge
waistband to pants

D

4. Fold the waistband in half, wrong sides together, encasing both side seams, and press the fold at the top to create a nice crease. **Fig. C**

5. Repeat Steps 3 and 4 to create 2 ankle cuffs.

6. Baste gathering stitches along the top raw edge of the harem pants. Pull the bobbin thread to gather the top edge of the pants to the same circumference as the yoga waistband.

7. Place the yoga waistband over the right side of the harem pants, aligning the raw edges of the waistband with the gathered edges of the pants. Stitch/serge, and remove the basting stitches. Press waistband up and seam down. **Fig. D**

8. Place the ankle cuffs over the ankle openings of the pants, right sides together and raw edges aligned. Stitch/serge. Press cuffs down and seam up.

Pleated Skirt

This adorable skirt closes the gap between preppy and trendy. It features three inverted box pleats and a flat-fronted waistband with elasticized back. Make it with knits for a casual look or with woven fabrics for a more structured look.

FABRIC AND NOTIONS

Use woven fabrics (quilting cotton, shirting, lightweight denim or stretch denim, satin, silk, twill, and chambray, 44″/45″). You can also use knit fabrics (cotton interlock, jerseys, rib knits) for a less structured look. Refer to Know Your Fabrics (page 7).

The amount of fabric you need to buy will vary depending on size, skirt length, and add-ons. Refer to the cutting instructions to determine the yardage. Always purchase at least ¼ yard extra to allow for fabric shrinkage.

Plan to use about ¾ yard for sizes 2T–5T, 1 yard for Girls' sizes 6–10, 1¼ yards for Tweens' sizes, and 1½ or more yards for Women's/Teens' sizes. Shorter skirts may use less fabric.

- ¾″-wide knit or non-roll elastic (enough for half of your Waist)
- Coordinating thread
- Rotary cutter and self-healing mat, or dressmaking shears
- Flexible measuring tape
- Water-soluble fabric marker

CUTTING

These directions are based on fabrics at least 44″ wide. Calculate the width of your skirt based on the Waist measurement (D). Base the length on the Skirt Length (N).

1. Cut 1 back waistband.

WIDTH: Waist measurement

HEIGHT: 3″

2. Cut 1 front waistband.

WIDTH: Waist measurement ÷ 2

HEIGHT: 3″

3. Cut 1 back skirt panel.

WIDTH: Waist measurement

LENGTH: Skirt Length measurement + ¼″

4. Cut 1 front skirt panel.

WIDTH: Front waistband width + 12″ for Girls/Tweens or + 18″ for Women/Teens

LENGTH: Skirt Length measurement + ¼″

5. Cut the ¾″-wide elastic.

WIDTH: Waist measurement ÷ 2, and then add 1″

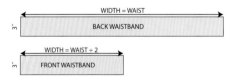

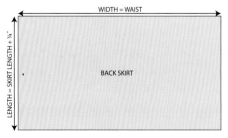

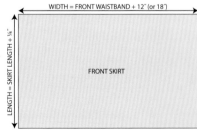

Assemble

All seams are ½˝.

1. Stitch the front waistband to the back waistband at the short ends, right sides together. **Fig. A**

Press seams open. Fold the band in half lengthwise, wrong sides together, and press. Set aside.

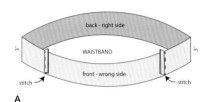

A

2. On the Skirt Front panel, make a small notch at the center of the upper edge as shown. Measure and mark another notch halfway between the side edge and the center on both sides.

Then mark notches the following distance away on either side of each of the first notches to total 9 notches—3 sets of 3 notches:

GIRLS'/TWEENS' SIZES: 2˝

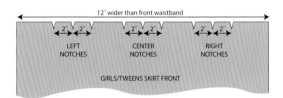

WOMEN'S/TEENS' SIZES: 3˝

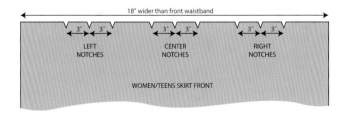

3. To make an inverted box pleat, fold the Skirt Front panel, wrong sides together, at the outer right-hand notch; press. Align the pressed fold with the center notch in that set; pin in place. Repeat the process with the left-hand notch so that the 2 folds meet in the center. Press well. Baste across the overlap, close to the raw edge.

> **TIP**
>
> *If sewing the Pleated Skirt out of knit fabrics, edgestitch ⅛˝ away from the fold of each pleat right after pressing to help the pleats keep their shape.*

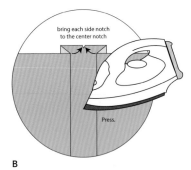

bring each side notch
to the center notch

Press.

B

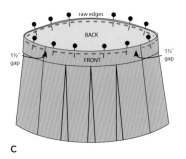

raw edges

BACK

1½"
gap

FRONT

1½"
gap

C

NOTE

Don't hem the box pleats shut. They should flare out at the bottom to create a nice A-line silhouette.

4. Repeat the previous step with the other 2 sets of notches to create 3 inverted box pleats on the Skirt Front. **Fig. B**

5. Stitch the pleated Skirt Front to the Skirt Back at the side edges. Finish the raw edges with a serger or zigzag stitch and press to the side.

6. Place the waistband over the finished skirt, right sides together, with raw edges aligned at the top, and with side seams also aligned. Pin all the way around. Stitch only along the back waistband from side seam to side seam. Then stitch along the front waistband, starting and stopping 1½″ away from each side seam. **Fig. C**

7. Using a safety pin or bodkin, feed the elastic through 1 of the gaps in the front waistband and maneuver it through the back waistband casing. Stitch down the end of the elastic at the side seam. Pull the elastic all the way through and out the opposite gap, and stitch that end at the seam. Stitch the gaps closed. Finish the waistband seam with a serger or zigzag stitch. Press the seam down and topstitch along the top of the skirt panels.

8. Hem the bottom of your skirt by folding the bottom edge toward the wrong side ¼″ and again another ½″. See Hemming Techniques (page 46) for alternative hems for knits.

Asymmetrical
Ruffled
Skirt

Our model is wearing an Asymmetrical Ruffled Skirt made with The Cottage Garden knits by Amanda Herring for Riley Blake Designs.

The sideways scoop of this asymmetrical skirt makes it flirty and fun, while the full ruffles add a touch of glamour.

FABRIC AND NOTIONS

Use knit fabrics only, such as cotton interlock, jerseys, rib knits, stretch velvet, or stretch velour, 58″/60″ wide. Make sure your knit fabric has at least 25% stretch. Refer to the stretch gauge diagram (page 9) in Know Your Fabrics.

The amount of fabric you need to buy will vary depending on size, skirt length, and add-ons. Refer to the cutting instructions to determine exact yardage. Always purchase at least ¼ yard extra to allow for fabric shrinkage. Plan on using about ¾–1 yard for Girls/Tweens and 1½ yards for Women/Teens. Plus sizes may require more fabric.

- ¾″-wide knit or non-roll elastic (enough for your Waist measurement)
- Coordinating thread
- Rotary cutter and self-healing mat, or dressmaking shears
- Flexible measuring tape
- Water-soluble fabric marker

CUTTING

These directions are based on fabrics at least 58″ wide. Remember that the maximum stretch of the fabric should always go from side to side, across the width of these panels. Calculate the skirt width based on your Hip measurement (E). Base the length on your Skirt Length measurement (N). You'll need your calculator for this one!

1. Cut 2 skirt panels:

WIDTH: Hip measurement ÷ 2, and then add 8″. For example, if my Hips measure 40″, the width of each fabric panel will be 40″ ÷ 2 = 20″ + 8″ = 28″.

LENGTH: Skirt Length measurement + 2″

2. Cut 2 ruffled hem bands:

WIDTH: Skirt panel width (from Step 1) × 2. Using the example from Step 1, if my skirt panel width is 28″, then my ruffle bands will be 56″ wide.

HEIGHT: 6″ high regardless of size

NOTE

If your ruffled hem band width is a little wider than the full width of your fabric, don't worry. Since the bands will be gathered and sewn onto the hem later, it is fine to cut these a bit short.

3. Cut 2 waistband panels.

WIDTH: Waist measurement (D) ÷ 2. For example, if my Waist measures 30″, the width of each waistband panel will be 30″ ÷ 2 = 15″.

HEIGHT: 3″ regardless of size

4. Cut the ¾″ elastic:

WIDTH: Waist measurement − 1″

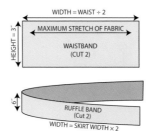

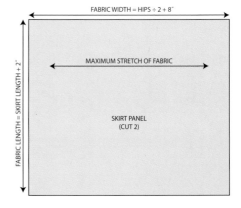

Assemble

All seams are ½″.

1. Place the skirt panels, right sides together, on a flat surface. Align all raw edges. Determine which end will be the skirt top and place a pin at the center point.

2. Divide your Waist measurement by 4. Add 1″ to this number for seam allowances and ease. For example, if my Waist measures 30″, then 30″ ÷ 4 = 7½″ + 1″ = 8½″. Place a pin at this measurement to the left and the right of the center mark.

3. Place another pin 7″ up from the bottom right corner of each skirt piece.

4. Using a water-soluble fabric marker, draw a slightly curved line from the top right pin to the bottom right pin. Draw another curved line from the top left pin to the bottom left corner. Lastly, draw the last curve from the bottom left corner to the bottom right pin, creating the asymmetrical hem. **Fig. A**

5. Cut both skirt panels along the curved lines drawn in Step 4. Discard the excess fabric or save for a future project. (These smallish pieces would work for pockets or skinny straps!)

6. With the skirt panels still right sides together, pin along both side edges. Stitch/serge along both sides. Turn skirt right side out. **Fig. B**

7. Refer to Ruffled Hem Band (page 140) to make and attach the ruffle to the bottom of the skirt.

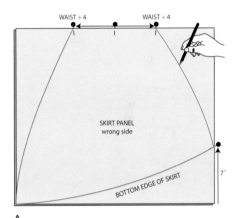

WAIST ÷ 4   WAIST ÷ 4

SKIRT PANEL
wrong side

BOTTOM EDGE OF SKIRT

7″

A

SKIRT PANEL
wrong side

B

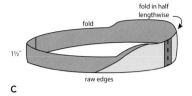

fold in half lengthwise

fold

1½″

raw edges

C

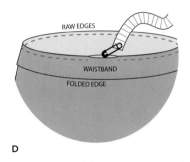

RAW EDGES

WAISTBAND

FOLDED EDGE

D

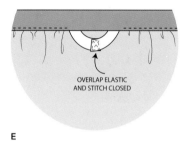

OVERLAP ELASTIC
AND STITCH CLOSED

E

8. Place the waistband panels right sides together, aligning all raw edges. Stitch/serge together along both short edges.

9. Fold the waistband in half, wrong sides together. Press the top fold to create a nice crease. **Fig. C**

10. Place the waistband over the right side of the skirt's top edge, aligning side seams and raw edges. Pin in place all around. Stitch/serge together, leaving a 1″ gap in the back for inserting the elastic.

11. Using a large safety pin or a bodkin, insert the elastic through the gap in the waistband, all the way around the casing, and out the same opening. Overlap the ends by ½″ and stitch closed. Stitch/serge the gap closed and press the seam down. **Fig. D & E**

Summer Fun

When summer is finally upon us, it's time to head to the beach or throw a fun pool party with your friends. Maybe you're taking a Caribbean cruise with the family or finally enrolling your kids in a ballet class.

Sheer fabrics, such as chiffon, organza, and georgette, and semi-sheer fabrics, such as voile, lawn, eyelet, gauze, and handkerchief linen, are perfect for all these summertime activities. In these six projects, you will learn techniques such as creating drawstrings, working with soft waistband elastics, and applying fringe or other fun trims.

Sheer fabrics, such as chiffon, organza, and georgette are perfect for summertime activities.

Beach Cover-Up

Our model is wearing a Beach Cover-Up sewn in Eyelet Mini Dot White Cotton fabric from Jo-Ann Fabric and Craft Stores.

Whether you are going to the beach, hitting the pool, or cruising around the Caribbean, you will need a lightweight swimsuit cover-up that is easy to sew and fits you perfectly.

FABRIC AND NOTIONS

Use lightweight or semi-sheer woven fabrics such as voile, lawn, eyelet, chiffon, or georgette. Refer to Know Your Fabrics (page 7).

The amount of fabric you need to buy will vary depending on size, cover-up length, and add-ons. Refer to the cutting instructions to determine the yardage. Always purchase at least ¼ yard extra to allow for fabric shrinkage. Allow about 1 yard for Girls/Tweens (2T to 10) and up to 2 yards for Women/Teens. Don't cut the fabric until you are absolutely sure you have enough!

- Coordinating thread
- Rotary cutter and self-healing mat, or dressmaking shears
- Flexible measuring tape
- Water-soluble fabric marker

CUTTING

These directions are based on fabrics at least 44˝ wide. Keep the direction of the print in mind when using directional fabrics. Calculate the cover-up width based on your Shoulder Width measurement (A). Base the length on your Dress Length measurement (L) or the distance from your shoulder to where you would like the cover-up to fall. Mid-thigh is the most common length. Grab your calculator because you will need it for this one!

1. Cut 2 cover-up panels following the formulas below to get the size:

WIDTH: Shoulder Width measurement + 6˝ for Girls/Tweens or + 12˝ for Women/Teens

LENGTH: Dress Length measurement (or measurement from your shoulder to where you would like your cover-up to fall) + 1¼˝ for seam and hem allowances

Label these as the front and back panels.

2. Cut 1 drawstring casing:

WIDTH: Cover-up panel width (from Step 1) × 2, and then subtract 2˝. For example, if my Cover-up panel width is 20˝, then my drawstring casing will be 20˝ × 2 = 40˝ − 2˝ = 38˝).

HEIGHT: 2˝ regardless of size

> **NOTE**
>
> *If the drawstring casing width you need is more than your full width of fabric, you may be able to cut it from the length of the fabric, or cut 2 pieces the width of your cover-up panel minus ½˝.*

Fabric Width = Shoulder Width + 6˝ (or 12˝)

Fabric Length

FRONT / BACK PANELS (CUT 2)

3. Cut a drawstring:

WIDTH: 1˝ for all sizes to yield a ¼˝ finished drawstring

LENGTH: Drawstring casing width (from Step 2) × 2. You most likely will have to cut 2 lengths and stitch them together.

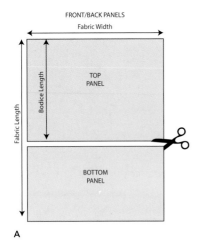

FRONT/BACK PANELS
Fabric Width

Bodice Length

Fabric Length

TOP PANEL

BOTTOM PANEL

A

Assemble

All seams are ½˝. Finish seam allowances with a serger or zigzag stitch.

1. Place the front and back panels on a flat surface. Determine which end will be the cover-up's top edge. Using a water-soluble fabric marker, place a mark at your Bodice Length measurement (K) from the top edge of both panels. Cut across both panels at the mark, and label the pieces "top front," "bottom front," "top back," and "bottom back." Set the back pieces aside for now. **Fig. A**

2. Cut each front panel in half vertically to make 4 panels. Set the 2 bottom front panels aside for now. **Fig. B**

3. Place the 2 top front panels right sides together. Mark 3˝ in from the top right corner on the top edge. Draw a diagonal line from the mark to the bottom right corner. Cut on the line and discard the excess small triangles. Open up both top panels to reveal mirrored center front neck openings. **Fig. C**

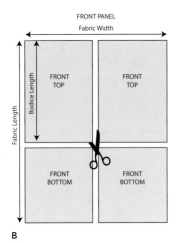

FRONT PANEL
Fabric Width

Bodice Length

Fabric Length

FRONT TOP

FRONT TOP

FRONT BOTTOM

FRONT BOTTOM

B

3˝

FRONT TOP

center front

C

4. Fold the top back panel through the width and finger-press the top center. Mark 3″ to the left and right of the center mark. Then mark 2″ down from the center mark. Using a water-soluble fabric marker on the wrong side of the fabric, join all 3 marks with a rounded curve to create the back neck opening. Cut out the neck opening and discard the excess fabric. **Fig. D**

5. Place the 2 top front panels on top of the top back panel, right sides together and outer raw edges aligned. Make sure the angled center front edges face each other, as shown. Stitch together along the shoulder seams. Finish the seams and press to the side. **Fig. E**

6. Open the top panels and hem the outer side edges and the entire neck opening edge with a ½″ hem allowance. You can serge or zigzag all raw edges first, and then fold ½″ to the wrong side and topstitch. Or, fold ¼″ to the wrong side, fold again another ¼″, and topstitch. Use the same hemming method throughout the entire garment. **Fig. F**

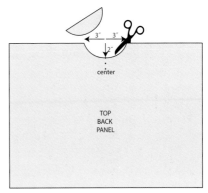

D

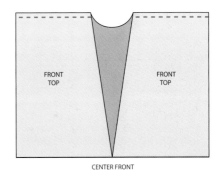

E

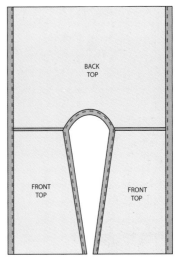

F

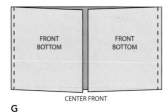

G

CENTER FRONT

7. Place the 2 bottom front panels right sides together on top of the bottom back panel, aligning the outer raw edges. Stitch together along both side seams. Finish the seams and press to the side. Hem the outer side edges and the bottom edge with the same technique as in Step 6. **Fig. G**

8. Pin the top edge of the bottom section to the bottom edge of the top section, right sides together and raw edges aligned. When you get to the sleeve openings on the sides, align both hemmed sleeve edges and pin them to the side seams in the bottom section. **Fig. H**

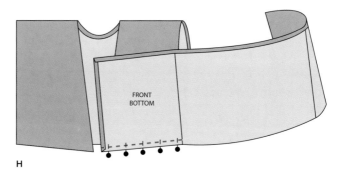

H

Make sure everything lines up perfectly, and then stitch together. Finish the waist seam allowance and press it down.

9. If your drawstring casing is 2 separate pieces, stitch them together at the short ends and press the seam open. Finish all 4 raw edges of the casing with a serger or zigzag stitch, and then press all 4 edges ½˝ to the wrong side. Topstitch along the short ends only. **Fig. I**

DRAWSTRING CASING

I

10. Center and pin the casing to the waist seam of the cover-up, aligning the short hemmed edges of the casing with the hemmed center front edge of the garment

Topstitch the casing in place ⅛″ from the top and bottom edges of the casing, leaving the front edges open for the drawstring. **Fig. J**

11. Place both drawstring pieces right sides together, aligning all raw edges, and then stitch across a short edge, creating a single long piece. Refer to Spaghetti Straps (page 138) to fold and press the drawstring piece so that it makes a ¼″-wide drawstring. Topstitch along the long open edge. Leave the 2 short edges unstitched for now.

12. Attach a safety pin or bodkin to an end of the drawstring and insert inside the casing, pulling it all the way though to the other end. Tie a knot at each end of the drawstring.

Make sure the drawstring ends are equal in length, and then place a couple of stitches at the center back of the drawstring casing to anchor it in place.

To wear your beach cover-up, use your fingers to pull and gather the casing along the drawstring, until it sits comfortably around your waist, and then tie a pretty bow at the front.

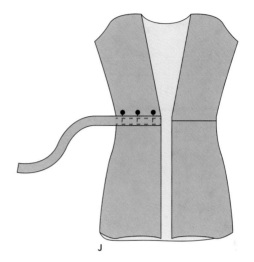

J

VARIATION: Add a cute pocket to the front of the cover-up, parallel to the front edges. Get ideas for cute pockets in Add-Ons (page 131).

Kimono-Style Robe

You'll be the envy of all your friends in your new Kimono-Style Robe. Whether you use it as a swimsuit cover-up in sheer fabrics or as a lightweight cocktail dress sewn in slinky knits, this will be your go-to piece this summer. It also works perfectly as a bathrobe in French terry or as a glamorous night-time robe in silks or satins.

FABRIC AND NOTIONS

Use lightweight fabrics that drape well, such as voiles, lawns, crepes, silks, satins, or shirtings. For a swimsuit cover-up, you can use a semi-sheer fabric such as cotton lace, handkerchief linen, or eyelet. For a warm and cozy bathrobe, try French terry cloth. This design also works well in light-weight, drapeable knits such as slinky knits and jerseys.

The amount of fabric you need to buy will vary depending on size, robe length, and add-ons. Refer to the cutting instructions to determine the yardage. Always purchase at least ¼ yard extra to allow for fabric shrinkage. You can make the entire robe from a single fabric or use a contrasting fabric for the sleeve bands, neck band, and waist sash. Plan on using at least 1½ yards total for Girls/Tweens, 2½ yards total for Women/Teens up to size Medium, and 3–3½ yards total for sizes Large and up. Shorter robes may use less fabric.

- Coordinating thread
- Rotary cutter and self-healing mat, or dressmaking shears
- Flexible measuring tape
- Water-soluble fabric marker

CUTTING

These directions are based on fabrics at least 44″/45″ wide. Calculate the width of your robe based on your Shoulder Width measurement (A). Base the length on your Dress Length measurement (L). Grab your calculator because you will need it for this one!

1. Cut 2 front panels and 1 back panel, following these formulas to get the size:

WIDTH: Shoulder Width measurement + 4″. For example, if my Shoulder Width is 16″, my fabric panels will measure 20″ wide.

LENGTH: Dress Length + 1½″ to allow for the ½″ shoulder seam and the 1″ hem

WIDTH = SHOULDER + 4″

LENGTH = DRESS LENGTH + 1 ½″

FRONT/BACK PANELS
(Cut 2 fronts and 1 back)

NOTE

If you are full-hipped, compare your Shoulder Width with your Hip measurement to make sure you'll have enough coverage in the front from the doubled-up front panels. If not, you may want to add a few inches to the panel width measurement.

2. Cut 2 sleeves as follows:

WIDTH: Bodice Length measurement (K) – 4″, and then multiply × 2. For example, if my Bodice Length is 18″, then my sleeve width will be 18″ – 4″ = 14″ × 2 = 28″.

LENGTH (SHOULDER TO ARM): 6″ for all sizes to yield a look like the robes photographed. If you prefer a longer or shorter sleeve, adjust this measurement.

3. Cut 2 sleeve bands.

WIDTH: Sleeve width (from Step 2)

LENGTH: 4″ for all sizes

4. Cut 2 neck bands.

WIDTH: 4″

LENGTH: Full width of fabric

5. Cut the sash.

WIDTH: 4″ for all sizes

LENGTH:

GIRLS/TWEENS: 2 strips × full width of fabric

WOMEN/TEENS: 2 strips × full width of fabric if Waist measurement is 42″ or less, or 3 strips × full width of fabric if Waist measurement is more than 42″

Assemble

All seams are ½˝. Press after each seam. Finish all seam allowances with a serger or zigzag stitch.

1. Place the 2 front panels right sides together. Measure and mark the Bodice Length measurement (K) down from the top of the panel along the right-hand side. Measure and mark 4˝ in from the top left corner for Girls/Tweens or 6˝ for Women/Teens. Draw a diagonal line to connect the marks, and then cut, discarding the small triangular pieces. **Fig. A**

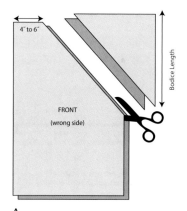

A

2. Place the 2 front panels over the back panel, right sides together, with the outer raw edges aligned and the diagonal cuts facing in. Pin and then stitch the shoulder seams. Finish the seam, and then press toward the front and topstitch. **Fig. B**

3. Finger-press the center of each sleeve width on 1 side. Place the sleeves on top of the opened robe panels, right sides together, and align the sleeve center with the shoulder seam. Stitch together. Finish the seams, and then press toward the sleeve and topstitch. **Fig. C**

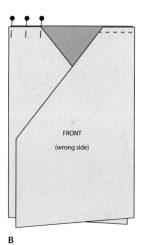

B

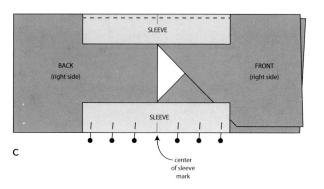

C

4. Place the entire garment right sides together, aligning raw sleeve edges, side edges, and underarm seams. Stitch from sleeve to hem, pivoting at the underarm. You may want to clip the seam allowances just to the stitching line at the pivot point. Finish the seams. **Fig.D**

TIP

If you serge this seam, you will not be able to pivot sharply. Instead, slightly round the corner at the underarm seam.

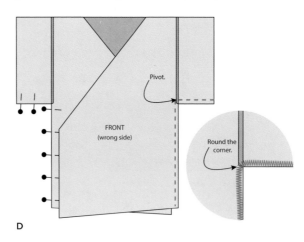

Pivot.

FRONT
(wrong side)

Round the corner.

D

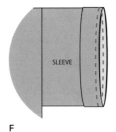

fold in half
wrong sides
together

FOLD

raw edges

E

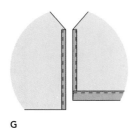

SLEEVE

F

G

5. Fold each sleeve band in half, right sides together, aligning the short ends, and stitch to make a loop. Press the seam open and then fold the band in half as shown, wrong sides together. Press the folded edge well to crease. **Fig.E**

6. Place each sleeve band over a sleeve, right sides together, aligning raw edges and seams. Pin all around and stitch. Finish the seams. Press the seam allowances toward the sleeve and the band away from the sleeve. Topstitch. **Fig.F**

7. Create a narrow hem up the straight front edges of your robe by pressing ¼″ toward the wrong side and then another ¼″. Topstitch close to the inner fold. Leave the angled edge unfinished for now. Also hem the bottom edge of the robe. Press ¼″ toward the wrong side and then another ¾″. Topstitch close to the inner fold. **Fig.G**

8. For Women's/Teens' sizes, place the 2 neck band pieces right sides together and stitch along a short edge. Press seam open. For all sizes, fold the neck band wrong sides together in half through the width and press well. Your band should now be 2″ wide.

9. Finger-press the center back of the robe along the neck edge. Find the center of the neck band, and pin it to the robe, aligning the long raw edge. When you reach the hemmed edges of the robe, measure ½˝ past the edge and trim off excess fabric. Open up the folded neck band and fold the extra ½˝ toward the wrong side of the neck band so it is flush with the hemmed edge of the front panel. Press well. Fig. H & I

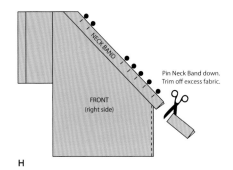

Pin Neck Band down.
Trim off excess fabric.

NECK BAND

FRONT
(right side)

H

10. Stitch the neck band to the robe and then finish the raw edges. Press the neck band out and the seam away from the neck band. Topstitch, continuing across the folded ends of the neck band. Fig. J

11. Stitch the sash pieces together along the short edges to create a single strip. Press seam(s) open. Fold the sash right sides together widthwise to make a 2˝ strip, and press well. Make a 45° cut at both ends. Stitch along the raw edges, leaving a small gap at the center for turning. Clip the ends within the seam allowance to avoid extra bulk. Fig. K

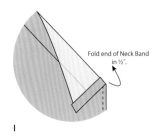

Fold end of Neck Band
in ½˝.

I

12. Turn the sash right side out through the gap and press well, making sure the points at the ends are nice and crisp. Topstitch close to the edge along the perimeter of the sash, closing the gap in the process.

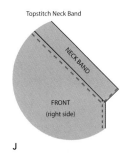

Topstitch Neck Band

NECK BAND

FRONT
(right side)

J

> **TIP**
>
> If you're afraid of losing the sash, here's a little trick:
> *Measure down the center back panel of your robe and finger-press at your natural waist. Pin the center of your sash to this point and stitch vertically to secure it at this spot. You will never lose it again!*

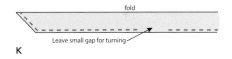

fold

Leave small gap for turning

K

VARIATION: Add a cute pocket to the front of the kimono-style robe, parallel to the front edges. Get ideas for cute pockets in Add-Ons (page 131).

Frilly
Sarong

This is by far the easiest project in this book! By using a single cut of fabric with no seams or closures, and adding fun trims, such as fringe or pom-poms, you will make a splash at your next pool party with this adorable sarong.

Learn to work with fringe.

FABRIC AND NOTIONS

Use lightweight sheer fabrics such as chiffon and georgette, or semi-sheer fabrics such as voile, lawn, eyelet, and gauze, 58″/60″ wide. Choose fabrics with moderate drape and a soft hand. Refer to Know Your Fabrics (page 7).

The amount of fabric you need to buy will vary depending on size, sarong length, and add-ons. Refer to the cutting instructions to determine the yardage. Always purchase at least ¼ yard extra to allow for fabric shrinkage. Allow ½ yard for Girls/Tweens and ¾–1 yard for Women/Teens.

- 1–2 yards (depending on size) of fringe, beaded, or pom-pom trim
- Coordinating thread
- Rotary cutter and self-healing mat, or dressmaking shears
- Flexible measuring tape

CUTTING

These directions are based on fabrics at least 58″ wide. Calculate the width of your sarong based on your Waist measurement (D). Base the length on your Skirt Length measurement (N). Grab your calculator because you will need it for this one!

Cut 1 sarong panel on the fold of fabric following these formulas to get the size:

WIDTH: Waist measurement (D) + 24″ for the ties, and then divide that number by 2, because you will cut the width on the fold of fabric. For example, if my Waist measures 30″, the width of the panel to be cut on the fold of fabric will be 30″ + 24″ = 54″ ÷ 2 = 28″.

LENGTH (AT THE LONGEST POINT): Skirt Length measurement (N) or wherever you want the longest point of the sarong to hit. Do not add to the length measurement; the hem allowance and the fringe length cancel each other out.

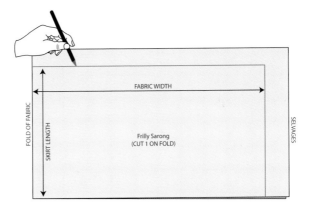

FABRIC WIDTH

FOLD OF FABRIC

SKIRT LENGTH

SELVAGES

Frilly Sarong
(CUT 1 ON FOLD)

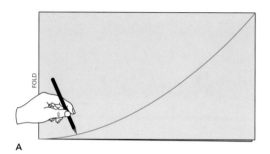

A

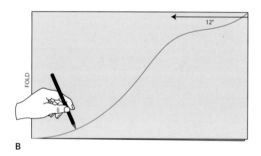

12"

B

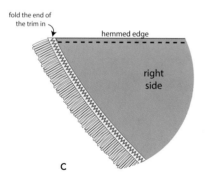

fold the end of
the trim in

hemmed edge

right
side

C

Assemble

All seams are ½".

1. With the sarong panel folded in half, draw a curve from the upper right corner to the lower left corner of the rectangle. You can make either a single curve or an S-curve. The S-curve will yield a narrower tie for the sarong, but either curve will work well with sheer fabrics. Cut along the line and discard the excess fabric. **Fig. A & B**

2. Hem the straight upper edge of the sarong with a narrow or rolled hem.

3. For stability, use a coordinating thread color to finish the curved edge with a serger or zigzag stitch.

4. Pin the trim to the right side of the curved edge of the sarong. At both ends, cut the trim ½" longer than the sarong and fold the ends under. Stitch the trim to the sarong with a wide zigzag stitch, backstitching at both ends. **Fig. C**

5. Tie the sarong around your waist with a single or double knot.

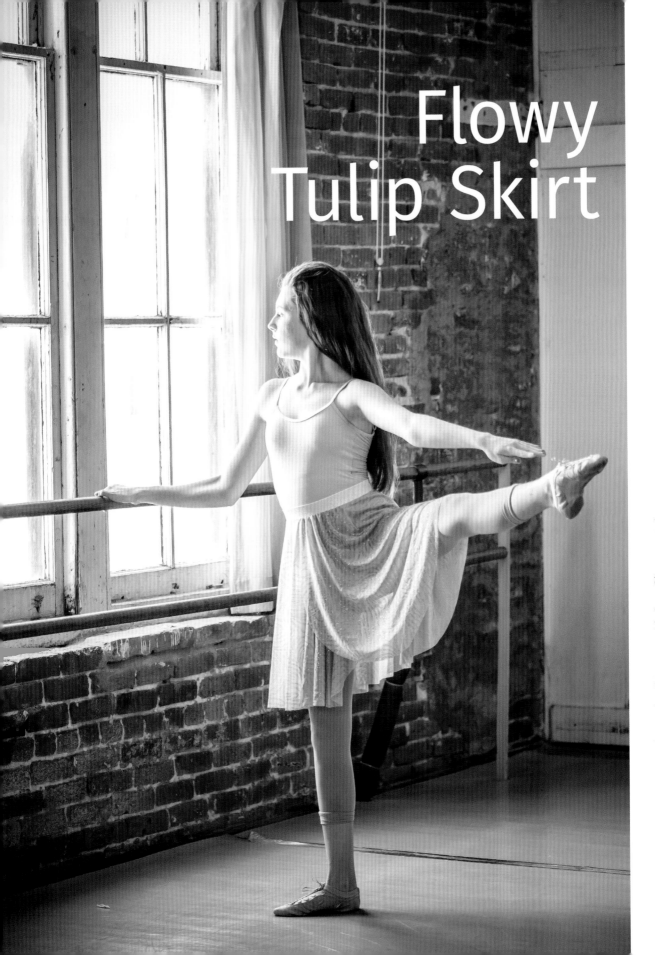

Flowy
Tulip Skirt

Perfect for dance class or to wear over leggings or tights for a night out, this classic wrap skirt has wonderful flow and drape because it is cut in a circle. The wavy hem resembles the edges of a tulip.

Perfect for dance class!

Using soft waistband elastic

FABRIC AND NOTIONS

To make this skirt as flowy as possible, use lightweight or sheer fabrics, preferably with a bit of stretch. I recommend slinky knits, ruffle knits, chiffon, georgette, crepe, stretch satin, or gauze.

The amount of fabric you need to buy will vary depending on size, skirt length, and add-ons. Refer to the cutting instructions to determine the yardage. Always purchase at least ¼ yard extra to allow for fabric shrinkage.

- 1½"- to 2"-wide soft waistband elastic in coordinating color, enough for your Waist measurement
- Coordinating thread
- Dressmaking shears
- Flexible measuring tape
- Water-soluble fabric marker

CUTTING

These directions are based on fabrics at least 56" wide. The Flowy Tulip Skirt is cut like a circle skirt, but wider at the waist so you can overlap the ends at the front to create the wrap effect. Calculate the width of your skirt based on your Waist measurement (D). Base the length on your Skirt Length measurement (N).

1. Cut 1 skirt panel following these formulas to get the size:

WAIST RADIUS (THIS INCLUDES THE FRONT OVERLAP): Waist measurement + 4" for Girls, + 6" for Tweens/Teens, + 8" for Women up to size 10, or + 10" for Plus-Sized Women; then divide this number by 6.28" (π* × 2).

π = pi (3.14)

For example, if my Waist measures 30", the radius of my skirt's waist will be 30" + 8" = 38" ÷ 6.28" = 6" (round to the nearest whole number).

LENGTH: Skirt Length measurement. Do not add length to this measurement. The waistband elastic and the seam/hem allowances cancel each other out.

To cut, fold the fabric in half right sides together so the selvages are aligned at the top. Mark the following with a fabric marker:

- Measure and mark the Skirt Length along the fold of the fabric from a raw edge.
- From that mark, measure and mark the Waist Radius. *This is the center of your skirt's waist.*
- From the center mark, measure and mark the Waist Radius along the fold on either side of and straight up from the center mark.
- Measure and mark the Skirt Length out from each Waist Radius mark on the fold.

There should be 4 marks along the fold of the fabric and 2 perpendicular to the fold.

- Draw a half-circle connecting the Waist Radius marks.
- Draw a larger half-circle connecting the Skirt Length marks.

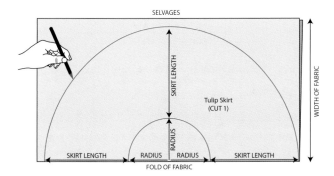

TIP

You can draw the half-circles by placing a pin at the center of the waist, tying a string around the pin and a fabric marker, and then marking the circle. Or you can measure from the center point out along the radius to place marks every 1″–2″, and then carefully join the marks.

- Cut on both drawn lines so you end up with a donut shape.
- Using the creased fold as a guide, cut open your "donut" on 1 side only, gradually curving the cut line as shown. This will be the front edge of the skirt.

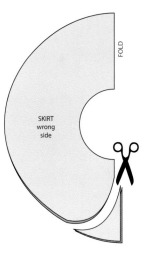

2. Cut the soft waistband elastic:

WIDTH: Waist measurement – 1″

Assemble

All seams are ½˝.

1. Hem all but the Waist Radius of the skirt using your desired method. See Hemming Techniques (page 46). I love doing a lettuce-edge rolled hem on tulip skirts because they accentuate the flowiness of this design.

2. Stitch the short ends of the soft waistband elastic together. Serge or zigzag the raw edges. Press the seam open to create less bulk, and then topstitch both sides close to the finished edge. **Fig. A**

A

3. Place the soft elastic waistband on a flat surface, right side out, with the seam at the center back. Place the skirt below the waistband and overlap the front edges so that the skirt's waist is 2˝ wider than the waistband on both sides, 4˝ total on each side. The best way to do this is to mark the center back with a pin. Align this pin with the center back seam of the waistband elastic, and then wrap the skirt edges toward the front and baste the overlap close to the edge. It is your preference as to which direction the overlap should run. **Fig. B**

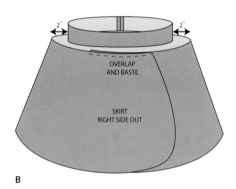

OVERLAP AND BASTE

SKIRT
RIGHT SIDE OUT

B

4. Quarter-mark the elastic waistband and the skirt's waist edge with pins. Right sides together, pin the elastic waistband to the skirt, aligning the quarter marks. As you pin, stretch the waistband elastic to fit the skirt, trying to stretch consistently so it will be even all the way around the skirt. Serge or stitch with a zigzag stitch and a ¼˝ seam allowance, stretching the waistband to fit as you stitch. **Fig. C**

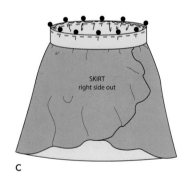

SKIRT
right side out

C

5. If your skirt is sheer, press the seam allowance up and topstitch it to the inside of the waistband with a wide zigzag stitch, so the seam is not visible. On opaque materials, you can let the seam allowance lie flat and the skirt fold over it, which will create less bulk at the waist.

Layered Handkerchief Skirt

Our model is wearing a Layered Handkerchief Skirt made with a beautiful Pintuck Diagonal Ribbon Cotton fabric courtesy of Jo-Ann Fabric and Craft Stores. The waistband is a 1¾″-wide silver soft waistband elastic, also from Jo-Ann Fabric and Craft Stores.

The asymmetrical pointed hem on the Layered Handkerchief Skirt makes this project whimsical and fun. You can make this skirt in just minutes using pre-purchased handkerchiefs or choose your favorite fabrics for a custom-made look.

FABRIC AND NOTIONS

To make this skirt as flowy as possible, use lightweight or sheer fabrics that drape well. I recommend eyelet, chiffon, organza, georgette, crepe, stretch satin, or gauze. You also can use pre-purchased square handkerchiefs or bandanas if they are large enough.

If you use yardage, the amount of fabric you need to buy will vary depending on size, dress length, and add-ons. Refer to the cutting instructions to determine the yardage. Always purchase at least ¼ yard extra to allow for fabric shrinkage. Allow 1½–2 yards for Girls'/Tweens' sizes and 2½ yards for Women's/Teens' sizes.

- 1½"- to 2"-wide soft waist-band elastic in coordinating color, enough for your Waist measurement
- Coordinating thread
- Dressmaking shears
- Flexible measuring tape
- Water-soluble fabric marker

CUTTING

These directions are based on fabrics at least 42″ wide. The skirt starts out with 2 equal squares of fabric with a circle cut out of the center. Calculate the radius of the circle based on your Hip measurement (E). Base the size of the square on your Skirt Length (N). Grab your calculator because you will need it for this one!

1. Cut 2 skirt squares following these formulas to get the size:

CIRCLE RADIUS: Hip measurement (E) ÷ 6.28 (π* × 2). For example, if my Hips measure 40″, the radius of my skirt's circle opening will be 40″ ÷ 6.28 = 6½″ (round up).

SIZE OF SQUARE: Skirt Length (N) × 2. For example, if my Skirt Length is 18″, my square size will be 36″ × 36″.

* π = pi (3.14)

> **NOTE**
>
> *If you want to use square handkerchiefs, bandanas, or scarves, a square with 25″–30″ sides works well for Girls'/Tweens' skirts; 40″–45″ works well for Women's/Teens'. The skirt will have a deliberately uneven hem due to the style, so it won't be exactly the same as the measured Skirt Length. If you feel like the skirt is too long after trying it on, you can always trim the skirt squares a few inches shorter all around and rehem.*

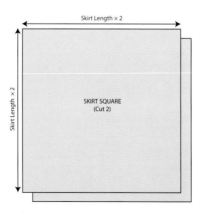

2. Mark and cut out the waist circles on 1 skirt square using the radius from Step 1.

- Fold each skirt square in half, creating a fold on 1 side. From the center of the fold, measure and mark the Circle Radius along the fold and perpendicular to the fold, as shown.

- Refer to the Flowy Tulip Skirt tip (page 89) for 2 ways to mark circles. Draw a half-circle connecting all of the circle radius marks.

- Cut on the drawn line and use this piece to cut the circle from the second skirt square.

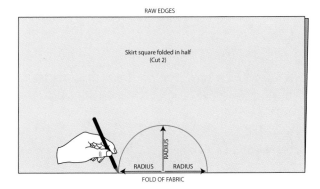

RAW EDGES

Skirt square folded in half
(Cut 2)

RADIUS

RADIUS   RADIUS

FOLD OF FABRIC

3. Cut the soft waistband elastic.

WIDTH: Waist measurement (D) –1˝

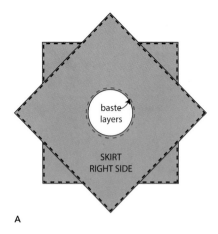

baste layers

SKIRT RIGHT SIDE

A

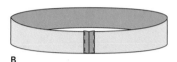

B

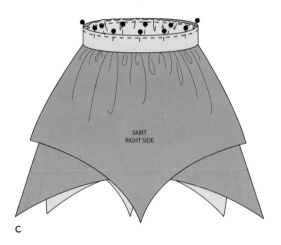

SKIRT RIGHT SIDE

C

> **NOTE**
>
> *The skirt's circle opening is much wider than the elastic so that it will fit over your hips.*

Assemble

All seams are ½″.

1. If you are using yardage, as opposed to pre-finished hankies, hem all outer edges of the skirt squares. You can finish the raw edges with a serger or zigzag stitch, press them ¾″ toward the wrong side, and then topstitch close to the inner edge, or use your preferred hemming method.

2. Place a skirt square on top of the other skirt square, both right sides up, aligning the inner circles. Rotate the top square 45° so you have 8 points at equal distances from each other. Baste around the inner circle opening, no more than ¼″ from the raw edge. **Fig. A**

3. Stitch the short edges of the soft waistband elastic together. If desired, serge or zigzag the raw edges to finish them. Press the seam open, and then topstitch both sides close to the finished edge. **Fig. B**

4. Quarter-mark the waistband and skirt's circle edge with pins, making sure the skirt's marks are perfectly aligned with the hem points. With right sides together, pin the waistband to the skirt, aligning the quarter marks and placing the waistband seam at the center back. As you pin, stretch the waistband elastic to fit the skirt, trying to stretch consistently so it will be even all the way around the skirt. Serge or stitch with a zigzag stitch and a ½″ seam allowance, stretching the waistband as you stitch. **Fig. C**

5. If your skirt is sheer, press the seam allowance up and stitch it to the inside of the waistband with a wide zigzag stitch, so the seam is not visible. On opaque materials, you can let the waist seam lie flat and the skirt fold over it, which will create less bulk at the waistband.

Pixie Skirt

Our little model is wearing a Pixie Skirt made with matte tulle, glitter tulle, ribbons, and soft waistband elastic from Jo-Ann Fabric and Craft Stores.

This is a fun project that you can get creative with, from the colors you choose to the way you layer it together. Use your imagination and create your own one-of-a-kind Pixie Skirt.

Mix tulle and ribbon strips.

FABRIC AND NOTIONS

These quantities are enough for an adult-sized skirt. You may need less for smaller sizes.

- 3 spools (25 yards each) of 6″-wide matte tulle

- 2 spools (15 yards each) of 3″-wide glitter tulle

- 3 spools (3 yards each) of ¼″-wide ribbon

- 1½″-wide soft waistband elastic in a coordinating color, enough to go around your waist

- Scissors or rotary cutter

- Coordinating thread

CUTTING

Calculate the length of the skirt based on your Skirt Length measurement (N). Base the width of the waistband on your Waist measurement (D).

1. Cut as many strips of matte tulle as your 3 spools will yield, or fewer for smaller sizes.

LENGTH OF STRIPS: Skirt Length measurement × 2. For the size 3T sample, we cut only 15 strips of each color (45 total) at 28″ long, but larger-sized skirts would look fuller with more strips. As you sew the skirt together, you can always add or subtract strips as you see fit.

2. Cut as many strips of glitter tulle as your 2 spools will yield.

LENGTH OF STRIPS: Length of the matte tulle strips – 4″. For the size 3T sample, we cut 10 strips of each color (20 total) at 24″ long.

3. Cut as many strands of ribbon as your 3 spools will yield.

LENGTH OF STRANDS: Length of glitter tulle strips – 4″. For the size 3T sample, we cut 7 strands of each color (21 total) at 20″ long.

4. Cut the soft waistband elastic.

WIDTH: Waist measurement – 1″

TIP

To save time when cutting the tulle and ribbon strips, cut a piece of cardboard to the length needed. Wrap the narrow goods around it, and then cut through all layers at each end. Discard any excess pieces that are too short.

Assemble

All seams are ½˝.

1. Fold each strip of tulle and glitter tulle in half lengthwise; finger-press to hold the shape if needed.

2. Working on a flat surface, place a folded strip of 6˝-wide matte tulle down with the fold at the top. Layer a different color 6˝-wide strip on top, overlapping half of the previous strip. Pin. Continue adding a new 6˝-wide strip every 3˝, alternating colors for a pleasing pattern, until you have used all the 6˝ strips. Then pin the 3˝-wide glitter tulle strips centered on the overlap of every third 6˝-wide strip.

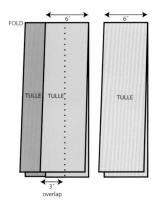
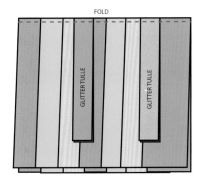

TIP

Don't attempt to assemble all the tulle strips before sewing. Once you have decided on a pattern, you can start with just a few strips. Keep the remaining strips in separate stacks and grab them as you need them. Keep adding strips until you feel you have enough fullness for the look you desire.

3. *Baste the strips together,* ¼˝ from the edge of the fold. Use your longest basting stitch because later you will gather this long train of strips.

4. Sew a second basting row ¼˝ below the first row. As you baste, add a strand of satin ribbon folded in half on top of every 3˝ glitter tulle strip. Align the fold of the ribbon with the folded edge of the tulle strips.

5. Pull the bobbin threads to gather the tulle skirt to 4˝ longer than your Waist measurement (D).

6. For extra reinforcement, sew a row of stitching on top of the gathering stitches. To flatten the bulk of the gathered strips, serge or sew a wide zigzag stitch along the gathered edge.

7. Right sides together, pin the tulle panel to the elastic. Leave ½˝ of elastic at the beginning and the end so you can stitch the elastic together into the waistband later without the bulk of the tulle in the way. Stretch the elastic slightly as you go. Serge or zigzag the skirt to the elastic, stretching as you go.

8. Fold the seam up and topstitch down to the inside of the waistband with a wide zigzag stitch.

9. With right sides together, serge or zigzag the short edges of the waistband together. Fold the seam allowance to the side and topstitch it down.

> **TIP**
>
> *When you sew on the elastic, try to stretch it at the same consistency so it is even all the way around the skirt.*

Layer On

Baby, it's cold outside, but that doesn't mean you have to throw fashion out the window. Some of the most sophisticated garments you'll see on the runway are often winter-wear pieces.

In this chapter, you will learn to sew with warm, plush fabrics, such as faux fur, minky, velvet, velour, and velveteen. There is even a project using laminated fabrics, for good measure.

You will learn to sew with warm, plush fabrics, such as faux fur, minky, velvet, velour, and velveteen.

Buttoned Shoulder Wrap

Our little model is wearing a Buttoned Shoulder Wrap made with Shaggy Cuddle Ivory and lined with Silky Satin, both from Shannon Fabrics.

There's no reason why you can't look fabulous even when you're all bundled up for the cold weather. This faux fur shoulder wrap, also called a stole, is the perfect winter accessory for that special holiday party or a night at the opera. Little girls love it too, for playing dress-up or attending fancy events.

FABRIC AND NOTIONS

For the outer wrap, use bottom-weight or plush fabrics such as twill, tweed, canvas, corduroy, denim, faux fur, minky/cuddle, fleece, velvet, velveteen, or velour. For the lining, use lining fabrics or silky satins.

The amount of fabric you need to buy will vary depending on size. Refer to the cutting instructions to determine the yardage. Always purchase at least ¼ yard extra to allow for fabric shrinkage.

Allow about ¼ yard each for the outer and lining fabrics for Girls'/Tweens' sizes (2T to 10) and ⅓ yard each for Women's/Teens' sizes. Don't cut the fabric until you are absolutely sure you have enough!

- 1˝- to 1½˝-wide button
- Coordinating thread
- Dressmaking shears (optional: embroidery scissors if using faux fur)
- Flexible measuring tape
- Water-soluble fabric marker
- Optional: Small pieces of lightweight fusible interfacing and tear-away or wash-away stabilizer

CUTTING

These directions are based on fabrics at least 54˝ wide. Calculate the width of your wrap based on your Shoulder Width measurement (A).

Cut 1 wrap panel from the outer fabric and 1 from the lining following these formulas to get the size:

WIDTH: Shoulder Width measurement × 2, and then add 4˝ for seam allowances and overlap. Or use the list below for general size guidelines.

HEIGHT:

GIRLS' SIZES 2–5: 30˝ wide × 6˝ high

GIRLS' SIZES 6–10: 36˝ wide × 8˝ high

TWEEN/TEEN SIZES 12–16: 40˝ wide × 10˝ high

WOMEN'S SIZES 2–10: 45˝ wide × 10˝ deep

WOMEN'S SIZES 12 AND UP: 50˝ wide × 10˝ high

> **TIP**
>
> *If you use plush fabrics, such as faux fur, make sure the pile (the length of the faux fur fibers) is pointing down, parallel to the height of the wrap, when you cut the fabric, not side to side. Cut the fabric with the wrong side up and use scissors (not a rotary cutter), being careful not to cut the edges of the fur as you cut the backing material. You can also use the edge of a razor blade or a pair of embroidery scissors. You want the fur to hang past the seam when you wear the wrap.*

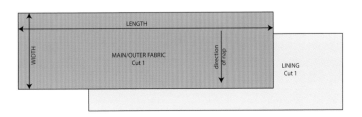

Assemble

All seams are ½″. No need to finish the seam allowances on this project.

1. Working from the wrong side, draw a curved line at the 2 short ends of the outer wrap, using a small plate for the Girls'/Tweens' sizes or a large dinner plate for the Women's/Teens' sizes. Cut on the lines and discard the excess fabric. Use the outer wrap as a template to round the corners of the lining.

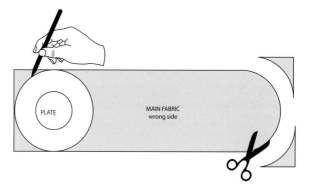

2. To add stability to the fabric where the buttonhole and button will go, fuse a small square of lightweight interfacing to the wrong side of the lining at both curved edges.

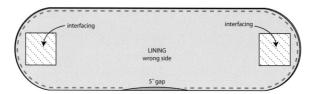

3. Place the outer and lining panels right sides together, aligning all raw edges, and pin all around. If you are using faux fur, tuck the overhanging edges of the fur inside, between both layers, so you will not stitch over them.

4. Stitch all around, leaving a 5″ gap on a long side for turning. Backstitch at the beginning and end to reinforce the stitches.

5. Clip the seam allowance at the curves so the seam will lie flat.

6. Turn the wrap right side out through the opening. Push out all the edges and smooth out the curves. Using a skewer or another small pointy object, pull through any fur that may have gotten stitched into the seam. Be careful not to rip the stitches.

7. Close up the gap by folding the seam allowance in and hand stitching the edges closed. You can also machine stitch it closed, if desired.

8. Place the wrap widthwise on a flat surface with the outer side facing up and the nap/pile pointing down. On the right-hand edge, mark 1″ in from the finished rounded edge, centered top to bottom. This is the outer edge of the buttonhole. From this mark, stitch a horizontal buttonhole to correspond to the width of your button.

9. Wrap the finished piece around your shoulders, where it is comfortable, and use the buttonhole as a guide to mark the position of the button on the other side of the wrap.

10. Stitch the button in place.

NOTE

If you are working with faux fur or other fabrics with pile, pin a small piece of tear-away or wash-away stabilizer over the fur before you stitch the buttonhole. It will help keep the pile from bunching up or getting caught in the machine.

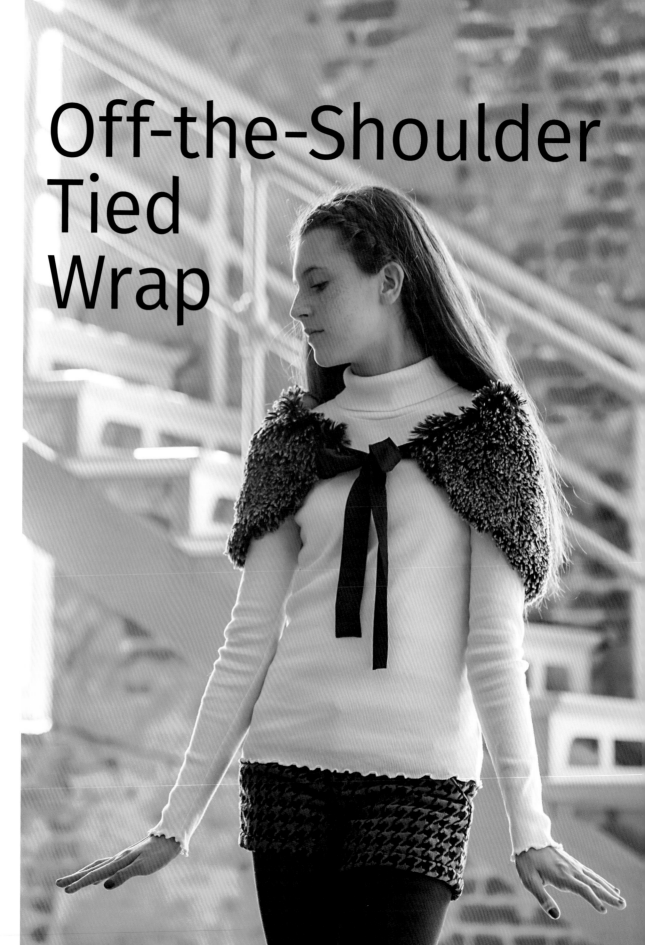

Off-the-Shoulder Tied Wrap

This elegant off-the-shoulder wrap will keep you warm during the cold nights, while letting your beautiful garment show through.

FABRIC AND NOTIONS

For the outer wrap, use bottom-weight or plush fabrics such as twill, tweed, canvas, corduroy, denim, faux fur, minky/cuddle, fleece, velvet, velveteen, or velour. For the lining, use lining fabrics or silky satins.

The amount of fabric you need to buy will vary depending on size. Refer to the cutting instructions to determine the yardage. Always purchase at least ¼ yard extra to allow for fabric shrinkage. Allow about ¼ yard each for the outer and lining fabrics for Girls'/Tweens' sizes (2T to 10) and ⅓ yard each for Women's/Teens' sizes. Don't cut the fabric until you are absolutely sure you have enough!

- 1 yard of ¾"-wide satin ribbon for Girls/Tweens or 1½ yards of 1"-wide satin ribbon for Women/Teens
- Coordinating thread
- Dressmaking shears (optional: embroidery scissors if using faux fur)
- Flexible measuring tape
- Water-soluble fabric marker

CUTTING

These directions are based on fabrics at least 54″ wide. Calculate the width of your wrap based on your Shoulder Width measurement (A). Base the length on your Elbow Length measurement (H).

1. Cut 1 wrap panel from the outer fabric following these formulas to get the size:

WIDTH: Shoulder Width measurement (A) × 2, and then add 1″ for seam allowances

LENGTH: Elbow Length measurement (H) + 1″ for seam allowances

If you are using a plush fabric, cut with the direction of the nap parallel to the length of the piece.

2. Cut 1 lining panel the same size as the outer panel.

3. Cut 2 strands of satin ribbon:

For Girls/Tweens, cut 18″ lengths of ¾"-wide ribbon.

For Women/Teens, cut 24″ lengths of 1″-wide ribbon.

> **TIP**
>
> *If using plush fabrics, such as faux fur, make sure the nap or pile is pointing down, parallel to the length of the finished piece, when you cut the fabric, not side to side. Do not use a rotary cutter because it will slice the edges off the fur. Embroidery scissors work well. Cut the fabric with the wrong side up, being careful not to cut the edges of the fur as you cut the backing material. You want the fur to hang past the seam when you wear the wrap.*

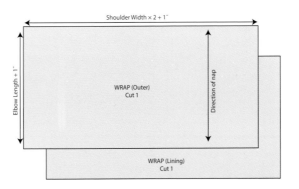

Assemble

All seams are ½″. No need to finish the seam allowances on this project.

1. Fold the main fabric in half through the Shoulder Width, right sides together. Mark the center of the folded layers with a pin at the bottom edge. Using a fabric marker, draw a curved line from the upper right corner to the pin. **Fig. A**

2. Cut on the line. (If using faux fur, cut 1 layer at a time, being careful not to cut through the pile of the fur.) Discard the cut-off corners. Use the wrap as a template to trim the lining piece to match.

3. Pin an end of a ribbon piece at each corner of the outer wrap piece, right sides together. Stitch the ribbon down ½″ from the corner. **Fig. B**

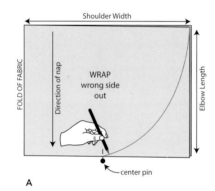

A

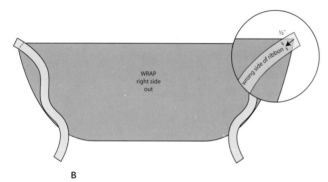

B

4. Place the main and lining panels right sides together, aligning all raw edges, and pin all around. Make sure the ribbons are sandwiched in between the layers. If you are using faux fur, tuck the overhanging edges of the fur inside, between both layers, so you will not catch them in the seam. Stitch all around, leaving a 5″ gap at the bottom of the wrap as shown for turning. Backstitch at the beginning and end to reinforce the stitches. **Fig. C**

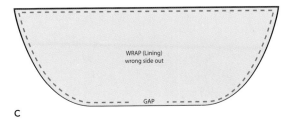

WRAP (Lining)
wrong side out

GAP

C

5. Clip the seam allowances at the curves and trim the corners within the seam allowance to allow the curves to lie flat and reduce bulk at the corners.

6. Turn the wrap right side out through the opening. Push out all the edges and smooth out the curves. Gently tug on the ribbons to make sure the seams are pulled out all the way. Using a skewer or another small pointy object, pull out any fur that may have gotten stitched into the seam. Be careful not to rip the stitches.

7. Close up the gap by folding the seam allowance in and hand stitching the edges closed. You can also machine stitch it closed, if desired.

8. Finish the edges of the ribbon by stitching a narrow hem with your sewing machine or a rolled hem with your serger. You can also heat seal the raw edge for a cleaner look.

9. Wear the wrap off the shoulders. Tie the ribbon into a pretty bow with long tails at the front.

Double-Breasted Capelet

This elegant capelet features a rounded Peter Pan collar and four large buttons on a classic double-breasted design.

Work with tweed, velvet, faux fur.

FABRIC AND NOTIONS

For the outer capelet, use bottom-weight or plush fabrics such as twill, tweed, canvas, corduroy, denim, faux fur, minky/cuddle, fleece, velvet, velveteen, or velour. For the lining, use lining fabrics or silky satins.

The amount of fabric you need to buy will vary depending on size. Refer to the cutting instructions to determine the yardage. Always purchase at least ¼ yard extra to allow for fabric shrinkage. Allow about 1¼–1½ yards each for the outer and lining fabrics for Girls'/Tweens' sizes (2T to 10) and 2–2½ yards each for Women's/Teens' sizes. You can also make the collar from a contrasting fabric, as we did here. Allow about ½ yard or a scrap at least 18″ × 18″. Don't cut the fabric until you are absolutely sure you have enough!

- ⅓ yard of fusible lightweight interfacing
- 4 buttons, 1″ wide
- Coordinating thread
- Dressmaking shears
- Flexible measuring tape
- Water-soluble fabric marker

CUTTING

These directions are based on fabrics at least 54″ wide. Calculate the length of your capelet based on your Elbow Length measurement (H). Refer to the cutting diagram (page 110). *Note: Because the cape goes from the neck over the shoulders and down, the finished length will be shorter.*

1. Cut 1 outer capelet, following this formula to get the size:

CAPELET LENGTH: Elbow Length measurement + 2″

> **NOTE**
>
> *If your fabric is only 54″ wide, the length of your capelet can be a maximum of only 24″. Wider fabrics will allow for longer capelets.*

To cut, fold the fabric in half right sides together so the selvages are aligned at the top.

- Measure in from the cut edge along the fold of the fabric and mark the Capelet Length with a fabric marker.
- From that mark, measure another 3″ along the fold for Girls/Tweens or 4″ for Women/Teens, and mark. This is the center of the neck opening, including the front overlap.
- Draw a larger half-circle connecting all of the outer marks.

> **TIP**
>
> *One way to draw the half-circles is to place a pin at the center of the neck opening mark, tie a string around the pin and a fabric marker, and then mark the circle.*
>
> *Another way is to use a measuring tape to place marks every 1″–2″, measuring from the center point out along the radius, and then carefully join all of these marks to form the two half-circles.*

- Cut both layers on both drawn lines so you end up with a donut shape.

- Using the creased fold as a guide, cut open the "donut" on 1 side only, from outer edge to inner edge. This will be the front edge of the capelet.

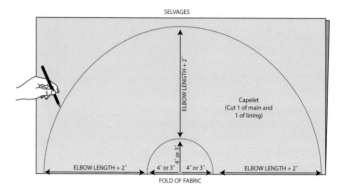

- Cut a small notch into the neck opening opposite the center front cut to denote collar placement.

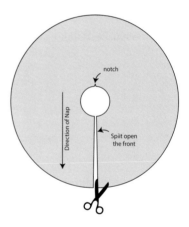

2. The collar will essentially be a much shorter version of the capelet. Repeat Step 1, using the same size neck opening and using the Collar Length below for the size you are making, to cut 1 outer collar.

COLLAR LENGTH: 3˝ for Girls/Tweens or 4˝ for Women/Teens

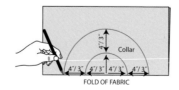

3. Fold the collar right sides together, aligning the front straight opening edges. Using a flexible measuring tape, measure and mark 3½″ in from the front opening along the inner circle. Cut along that mark, shortening the collar by 3½″ equally on each side. The angle of your cut depends on the look you are after. You can make a straight cut for a preppy look or a diagonal cut for a more open look. There is no right or wrong.

Using a small rounded object as a template, trim the outer corners of the collar. Discard the corner pieces.

> **TIP**
>
> *To get the rounded corners perfectly even, fold the collar in half, aligning all edges, and cut both sides at the same time.*

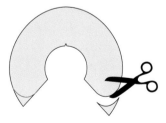

4. Cut 1 capelet lining from the lining fabric, using the capelet as a template.

5. Follow the manufacturer's instructions to fuse lightweight interfacing to the wrong side of a square of lining material cut slightly larger than the outer collar. Use the finished outer collar as a template to cut 1 collar lining.

Assemble

All seams are ½". Backstitch at the beginning and end of all seams. No need to finish seam allowances on this project since there are no exposed seams.

1. Place the collar lining and outer collar right sides together, and pin around the outer curve.

Stitch together, leaving the inner curve unstitched.

Notch the seam allowances around the outer curve and trim the corners; then turn right side out. Press edges well and topstitch around the outer curve. Baste the inner curve layers together to prevent shifting. **Fig. A & B**

2. With all right sides facing up, align the small notch on the collar with the small notch on the neck opening of the outer capelet. Pin the basted edges of the collar along the curved neck opening of the capelet. Baste in place. The open area will be the front overlap. **Fig. C**

3. Fuse 2 small squares of lightweight interfacing to the wrong side of the capelet lining, at both top corners, to add support for buttonholes and buttons. **Fig. D**

4. Place the lining and the outer capelet right sides together, with the collar sandwiched between. Make sure all of the raw edges are perfectly aligned, and then pin all around.

Starting about 2½" to the left of the center back crease, begin stitching the layers together. Stitch around the bottom edge, up the straight front edge, around the curved neck opening, down the other front edge, and finally along the bottom edge of the capelet, ending about 5" away from the starting stitches, leaving a gap for turning. **Fig. E**

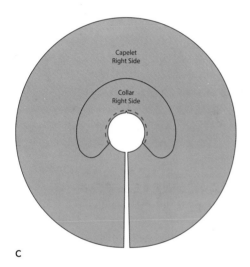

A

B

Collar
Right Side

Baste

Capelet
Right Side

Collar
Right Side

C

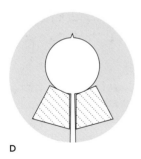

D

5. Turn the capelet right side out through the opening. Use a blunt object, such as a bone folder or a wooden chopstick, to push out the corners so they are nice and square, and gently tug on the collar to make sure it is pulled out all the way.

Topstitch along all of the outer sewn edges, closing the gap.

6. Overlap the front straight edges of the capelet, left over right as shown, so that the left front edge of the capelet meets the right rounded edge of the collar and vice versa.

Measure ½˝ down from the top edge and ½˝ over from the front straight edge of the capelet to mark placement for the top right buttonhole. Mark a ¾˝-wide horizontal buttonhole starting at that spot.

Mark the bottom right buttonhole 2½˝ below the first buttonhole marking.

The 2 left buttonholes should mirror the positioning of those on the right, keeping in mind the left edge of the capelet (which is now underneath). Make sure all buttonhole markings are perfectly aligned, and then stitch. **Fig. F**

7. Use the buttonholes as a guide to mark where to stitch the 4 buttons on the other side of the capelet.

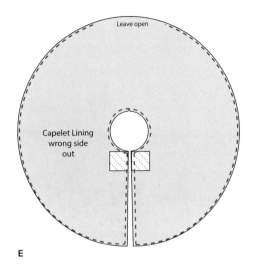

E

TIP

The best way to make sure the left buttonholes perfectly mirror those on the right is to stitch the two right buttonholes first, cut open their centers, and then fold the edge of the capelet over to the left, exposing the lining and aligning the top edge. Use the previous buttonholes as a guide to mark the position of the left buttonholes.

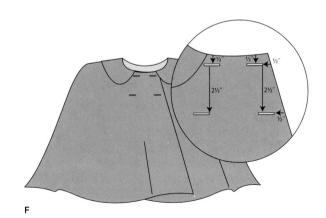

F

Shrug/Bolero

Make this fashionable Bolero vest out of plush fabrics for the winter months or from lighter fabrics for the warmer months. It looks adorable layered over a simple tee or a dressy blouse.

FABRIC AND NOTIONS

Use bottom-weight woven fabrics such as twill, denim, corduroy, canvas, velvet, velour, or velveteen.

> **NOTE**
>
> *This garment is unlined, so do not use any fabrics that would require a lining, such as any textile with a rough or unfinished wrong side.*

The amount of fabric you need to buy will vary depending on size. Refer to the cutting instructions to determine the yardage. Always purchase at least ¼ yard extra to allow for fabric shrinkage. Allow about 1 yard for Girls'/Tweens' sizes (2T to 10) and 1½ yards each for Women's/Teens' sizes. Don't cut the fabric until you are absolutely sure you have enough!

- ½″-wide knit or non-roll elastic (about ½–¾ yard for Girls/Tweens or 1–1½ yards for Women/Teens)
- Coordinating thread
- Rotary cutter and self-healing mat, or dressmaking shears
- Flexible measuring tape
- Water-soluble fabric marker

CUTTING

These directions are based on fabrics at least 44″ wide. Calculate the width of your Shrug based on your Shoulder Width measurement (A). Base the length on your Bodice Length measurement (K).

1. Cut 1 front panel following these formulas to get the size:

WIDTH: Shoulder Width measurement + 6″ for Girls/Tweens or 8″ for Women/Teens

LENGTH: Bodice Length measurement + 1½″ for seam and hem allowances

2. Cut 1 back panel:

WIDTH: Shoulder Width measurement + 3″ for Girls/Tweens or 4″ for Women/Teens

LENGTH: Bodice Length measurement + 1½″ for seam and hem allowances

3. Cut 1 drawstring:

WIDTH: 2″

LENGTH: 25″ for Girls/Tweens or 37″ for Women/Teens

4. Cut 1 length of elastic:

LENGTH: Waist measurement − 1″

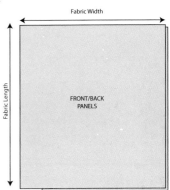

Assemble

All seams are ½". Press after each seam. Finish seam allowances with a serger or zigzag stitch.

1. Fold the back panel in half through the width, aligning all raw edges. On the top edge of the panel, mark 3" out from the center fold as shown. Then mark 2" down from the top corner of the center fold. With a water-soluble marker, draw a gentle curve from mark to mark, creating the back neck opening. **Fig. A**

2. Cut the front panel in half vertically as shown. Place the panels right sides together with a short end at the top. Along the upper edges, mark in 4½" from the top left corner for Girls/Tweens or 5" for Women/Teens. Draw a diagonal line from that mark to the bottom left corner. Cut on the line and discard the excess. Open the top panels to reveal mirrored front neck openings. **Fig. B**

3. Place the 2 front panels on top of the back panel, with right sides together and with neck openings and all raw edges aligned. Stitch together along the shoulder seam. Finish the seams and press to the side. **Fig. C**

4. Hem the neck opening edge with a ½" hem allowance. You can serge or zigzag all raw edges first, and then fold ½" to the wrong side and topstitch. Or fold ¼" to the wrong side, and then fold again another ¼" and topstitch. Use the same hemming method throughout this garment. Leave the bottom edges and side edges unstitched for now. **Fig. D**

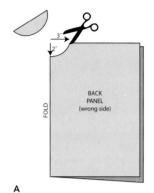

A

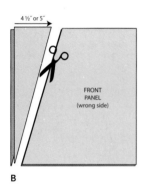

B

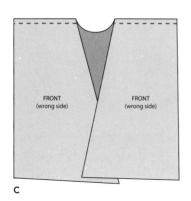

C

5. Finish the raw edges along both sides of the Shrug/Bolero, front and back. From the outer edge of the shoulder seam, on both sides, measure down 6″ (Girls' sizes 2–5), 8″ (Girls' sizes 6–10), or 10″ (Women's/Teens' sizes) for the arm opening. Place a pin at both sides.

> **NOTE**
>
> *Plus-size women may need a larger arm opening. Use a tape measure and adjust the opening as needed to ensure a perfect fit.*

6. Fold the Shrug right sides together at the shoulders, aligning all outer edges and matching the pins at the sides. Starting at the pin, stitch the sides closed down to the hem. Backstitch a couple of times at the beginning and end to reinforce the stitches. Press the seam open. **Fig. E**

7. Press the edges above the pin ½″ to the wrong side and topstitch from the right side of the garment, ¼″ away from the edge, finishing the sleeve opening. Stitch a straight line where the seams meet at the bottom of the arm opening. **Fig. F**

8. Topstitch ¼″ on either side of each side seam, making sure to catch the seam allowance underneath. Not only does this give a nice decorative touch to the garment, but it will help keep the seam allowance flat inside the casing.

9. To create the elastic casing, fold the bottom edge of the Shrug/Bolero ¼″ toward the wrong side and press well. Fold again another ¾″ and press well. Topstitch close to the upper fold, backstitching at the beginning and end to reinforce your stitches.

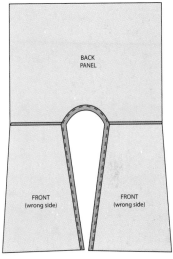

D

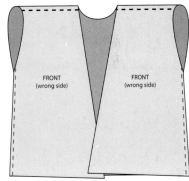

E

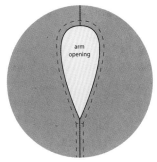

F

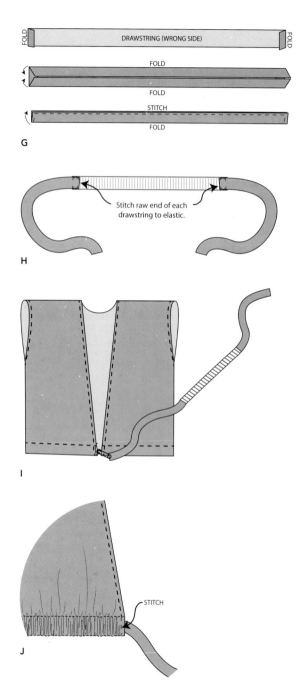

10. To make the drawstring, fold each short edge in toward the wrong side ½″. Fold the entire strip in half lengthwise, and then press to create a crease down the center. Open the strip and then fold the 2 long edges in toward the wrong side until they meet at the center crease. Press the edges well. Fold the entire piece in half at the crease, encasing the long raw edges. The drawstring should be ½″ wide at this point. Topstitch along the long open edge and down the 2 short edges. Cut the drawstring in half to yield 2 pieces 12″ long for Girls/Tweens or 18″ long for Women/Teens. Stitch the raw edge of the drawstrings to each end of the elastic. **Fig.G & H**

11. Use a safety pin or bodkin to help guide the elastic through the casing, pulling it all the way though to the other end.

12. Make sure the drawstring ends are equal in length on the outside, with the elastic fully encased within the casing. Stitch vertically over the previous front-edge stitches to anchor the elastic in place inside the casing. Distribute the fabric evenly along the elastic. **Fig.I & J**

VARIATION: Add a cute pocket to the front of the Shrug/Bolero, parallel to the front edges. Get ideas for cute pockets in Add-Ons (page 131).

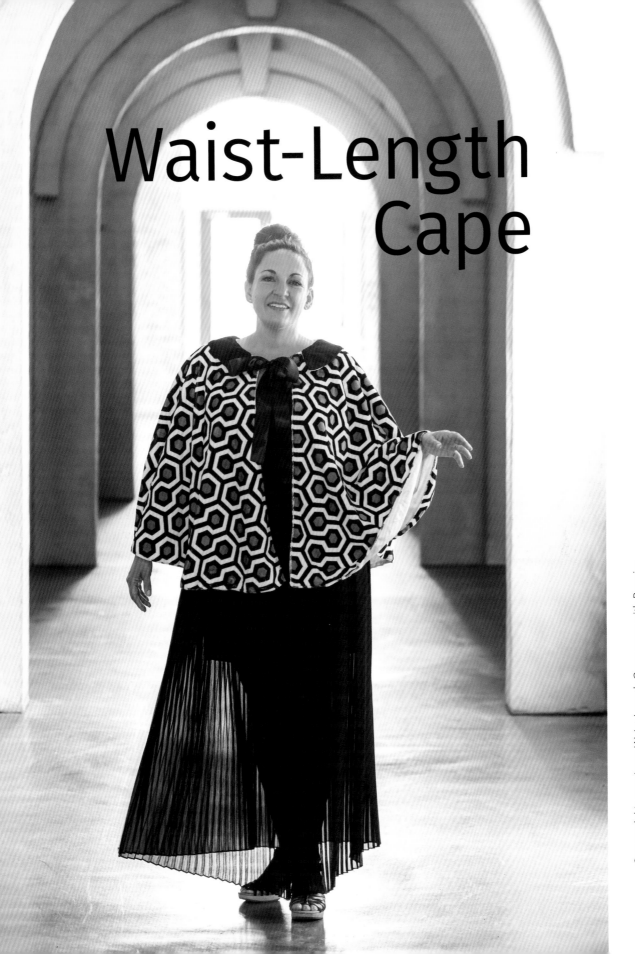

Waist-Length Cape

Our model is wearing a Waist-Length Cape sewn with Premier Favo Cuddle Black/Oyster/Snow fabric from Shannon Fabrics. The lining is Silky Satin in white, also from Shannon Fabrics.

Featuring an adorable Peter Pan collar and long ribbon ties, our Waist-Length Cape is perfect for making a fashion statement on a chilly night or for playing dress-up.

FABRIC AND NOTIONS

For the outer cape, use bottom-weight or plush fabrics such as twill, tweed, canvas, corduroy, denim, faux fur, minky/cuddle, fleece, velvet, velveteen, or velour. For the lining, use lining fabrics or silky satins.

The amount of fabric you need to buy will vary depending on size. Refer to the cutting instructions to determine the yardage. Always purchase at least ¼ yard extra to allow for fabric shrinkage. Allow about 1¼–1½ yards each for the outer and lining fabrics for Girls'/Tweens' sizes (2T to 10) and 2–2½ yards each for Women's/Teens' sizes. Don't cut the fabric until you are absolutely sure you have enough!

- ⅓ yard of fusible lightweight interfacing
- 1"- to 1½"-wide satin or grosgrain ribbon: 1 yard for Girls/Tweens, 2 yards for Women/Teens
- Coordinating thread
- Rotary cutter and self-healing mat, or dressmaking shears
- Flexible measuring tape
- Water-soluble fabric marker

CUTTING

These directions are based on fabrics at least 58" wide. Calculate the length of your cape based on your Arm Length measurement (G).

1. Cut 1 outer cape following these formulas to get the size:

CAPE LENGTH: Arm Length measurement + 2"

> **NOTE**
>
> *If your fabric is only 54" wide, the length of your cape can be a maximum of only 24". Wider fabrics will allow for longer capes.*

To cut, fold the fabric in half, right sides together, so the selvages are aligned at the top.

- Measure in from the cut edge along the fold of the fabric and mark the Cape Length with a fabric marker.
- From that mark, measure and mark over on the fold another 2" for Girls/Tweens or 3" for Women/Teens. This is the center of the neck opening.
- From the center mark, measure and mark along the fold and up, perpendicular to the fold, the same 2" or 3".
- Finally, from both neck opening marks, measure and mark the Cape Length along the fold and up from the neck.
- Draw a half-circle connecting all of the neck opening marks.
- Draw a larger half-circle connecting all of the outer marks.

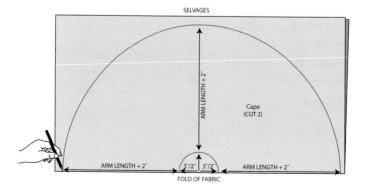

- Cut both layers on both the drawn lines so you end up with a donut shape.

- Using the creased fold as a guide, cut open the "donut" on 1 side only, from the outer to the inner edge. This will be the center front edge of the cape.

- Cut a small notch into the neck opening opposite the center front cut to denote collar placement.

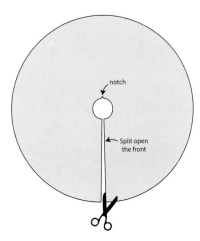

TIP

One way to draw the half-circles is to place a pin at the center of the neck opening mark, tie a string around the pin and the fabric marker, and then mark the circle.

Another way is to use a measuring tape to place marks every 1˝–2˝, measuring from the center point out along the radius, and then carefully join all of these marks to form the two half-circles.

2. The collar will essentially be a much shorter version of the cape. Repeat Step 1, using the same size neck opening and using the Collar Length below for the size you are making, to cut 1 outer collar.

COLLAR LENGTH: 3˝ for Girls/Tweens or 4˝ for Women/Teens

Cut another ½˝ off both front straight edges so that the collar will be slightly narrower than the cape.

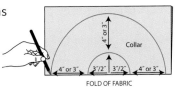

3. Cut 1 cape lining, using the outer cape as a template.

4. Follow the manufacturer's instructions to fuse lightweight interfacing to the wrong side of a square of lining material cut slightly larger than the outer collar. Use the finished outer collar as a template to cut the lining.

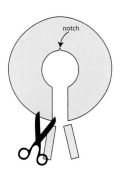

5. Cut 2 strands of ribbon for the size you are making:

LENGTH: 12˝ for Girls/Tweens or 18˝ for Women/Teens

Assemble

A

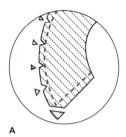

Collar
Right Side

B

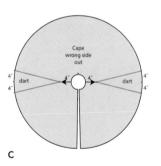

Cape
wrong side
out

4˝
4˝   dart   4˝   4˝   dart   4˝
4˝   4˝

C

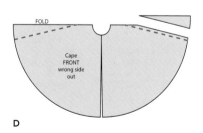

FOLD

Cape
FRONT
wrong side
out

D

All seams are ½˝. Backstitch at the beginning and end of all seams. No need to finish the seam allowances on this project since there are no exposed seams.

1. Place the collar lining and outer collar right sides together, and pin around the outer curve.

Stitch together, leaving the inner curve unstitched. Notch the seam allowances around the outer curve, trim the corners, and then turn right side out. Press edges well and topstitch around the outer curve. Baste the inner curve layers together to prevent shifting. **Fig. A & B**

2. Lay the outer cape out in a single layer, wrong side up. Mark, pin, or finger-press the halfway points between the center back and center front on the neck opening and the cape's outer edge. Measure 4˝ out from the neck opening on each side to mark the top of the shoulder with a fabric marker. At the outer edge of the cape, measure and mark 4˝ to each side of the halfway point. Draw straight lines between the shoulder point and the outer marks to create triangular side darts, as shown. **Fig. C**

3. Fold the cape in half, right sides together, through the shoulder points, aligning the dart marks. Pin and stitch on the dart lines. Trim the excess fabric ½˝ away from the stitching lines and press the seams toward the back. **Fig. D**

4. Repeat Steps 2 and 3 to add darts to the cape lining.

5. With all right sides facing up, align the small notch on the collar with the small notch on the neck opening of the outer cape. Pin the basted edges of the collar along the curved neck opening of the cape, ending about 1˝ away from the front of the cape on both sides. Baste in place.

6. Finish a raw end of each strand of ribbon. Pin the other raw end of each ribbon to the front straight edges of the cape 1″ below the top edge, aligning raw edges. Baste in place. Fig. E

7. Place the lining and the outer cape right sides together, with the collar and ribbons sandwiched between. Make sure all of the raw edges are perfectly aligned, and then pin all around. Starting about 2½″ to the left of the center back crease, begin stitching the layers together. Stitch around the bottom edge, up the straight front edge, around the curved neck opening, down the other front edge, and then finally along the bottom edge of the cape, ending about 5″ away from the starting stitches, leaving a gap for turning. Fig. F

8. Turn the cape right side out through the opening. Use a blunt object, such as a bone folder or a wooden chopstick, to push out the corners so they are nice and square, and gently tug on the collar to make sure it is pulled out all the way. Topstitch along all of the outer sewn edges, closing the gap.

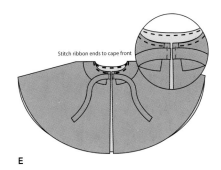

Stitch ribbon ends to cape front

E

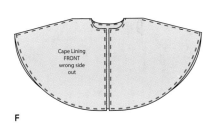

Cape Lining
FRONT
wrong side
out

F

VARIATION: Add a cute pocket to the front of the cape, parallel to the front edge. Get ideas for cute pockets in Add-Ons (page 131).

Reversible
Rain Poncho

Our teen model is wearing a Reversible Rain Poncho made with laminated cottons from Riley Blake Designs. It also features a Circular Pocket (page 135). Our girl model's Rain Poncho is made with laminated cottons from the Lush collection by Patty Young for Michael Miller Fabrics.

While stitching up this versatile rain poncho, you will learn how to work with laminated fabrics, as well as how to create darts, plackets, and buttonholes. A rain poncho is better than a raincoat because it can cover your backpack, purse, or bag while showing off your style.

FABRIC AND NOTIONS

Use laminated cottons, oilcloth, or vinyl with a nondirectional print, at least 54″ wide. You will need 2 different prints to make your rain poncho fully reversible.

The amount of fabric you need to buy will vary depending on size, poncho length, and add-ons. Refer to the cutting instructions to determine the yardage. Always purchase at least ¼ yard extra to allow for fabric shrinkage. Allow about 1¼–1½ yards each of the main/outer and lining/contrasting fabrics for Girls'/Tweens' sizes (2T to 10) and 2–2½ yards each for Women's/Teens' sizes. Don't cut the fabric until you are absolutely sure you have enough!

- 5 or 10 buttons ¾″ wide for Girls'/Tweens' sizes (2T–10) or 7 or 14 buttons 1″ wide for Women's/Teens' sizes (You will need buttons for both sides if you want the poncho to be fully reversible.)

- Coordinating thread

- Rotary cutter and self-healing mat, or dressmaking shears

- Flexible measuring tape

- Water-soluble fabric marker

- Buttonhole foot for the sewing machine

- Hair clips or small binder clips (I like to use these instead of pins for laminated fabrics because they will not leave holes.)

Optional: A Teflon or nonstick sewing machine foot can be helpful when sewing laminated fabrics, but it is not necessary. If the material sticks when you try to sew it, try putting clear adhesive tape on the bottom of your presser foot to help it slide over the material.

CUTTING

These directions are based on fabrics at least 54″ wide. Calculate the length of your poncho based on your Arm Length measurement (G). *Note: Because the cape goes from the neck over the shoulders and down, the finished length will be shorter.*

1. Cut 1 outer/main poncho from the laminated fabric following the instructions below:

PONCHO LENGTH: Arm Length measurement + 2″

> **NOTE**
>
> *Because most laminated fabrics are 54″ wide, the length of your poncho can be a maximum of only 24″. Wider fabrics will allow for longer ponchos.*

To cut, fold the laminated fabric in half, right sides together, so the selvages are aligned at the top.

- Measure in from the cut edge along the fold of the fabric and mark the Poncho Length with a fabric marker.

- From that mark, measure and mark over on the fold another 2″ for Girls/Tweens or 3″ for Women/Teens. This is the center of the neck opening.

- From the center mark, measure and mark along the fold *and* up, perpendicular to the fold, the same 2″ or 3″.

- Finally, from both neck opening marks, measure and mark the Poncho Length along the fold *and* up from the neck.

- Draw a half-circle connecting all of the neck opening marks.

- Draw a larger half-circle connecting all of the outer length marks.

TIP

One way to draw the half-circles is to place a pin at the center of the neck opening mark, tie a string around the pin and the fabric marker, and then mark the circle.

Another way is to use a measuring tape to place marks every 1″–2″, measuring from the center point out along the radius, and then carefully join all of these marks to form the two half-circles.

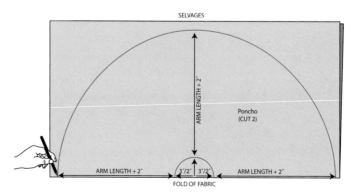

- Cut on both drawn lines so you end up with a donut shape.

- Using the creased fold as a guide, cut open the "donut" on 1 side only, from outer edge to inner edge. This will be the center front edge of the poncho.

- Cut a small notch into the neck opening opposite the center front cut to denote hood placement.

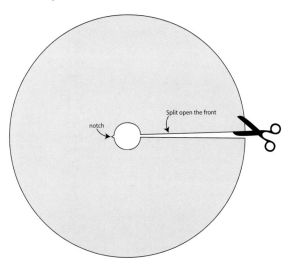

notch
Split open the front

2. Cut 1 poncho lining, using the outer/main poncho as a template.

3. Cut 2 button plackets from the main/outer fabric and 2 from the lining/contrasting fabric:

WIDTH: 2½" for Girls/Tweens or 3" for Women/Teens

LENGTH: Arm Length + 2"

On most kids' ponchos, you should be able to cut the 2 plackets from the same width of fabric.

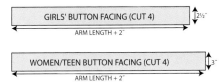

GIRLS' BUTTON FACING (CUT 4)
2½"
ARM LENGTH + 2"

WOMEN/TEEN BUTTON FACING (CUT 4)
3"
ARM LENGTH + 2"

4. To draw the hood piece, fold the outer fabric in half, right sides together, and mark a rectangle on the wrong side of the outer/main fabric, following the top width and height below. Then adjust the width of the bottom rectangle as shown, and join the top and bottom lines with an angled line as shown.

FOR GIRLS/TWEENS (SIZES 2T TO 10):

TOP WIDTH: 12"

HEIGHT: 14"

BOTTOM WIDTH: 8"

FOR WOMEN/TEENS (SIZES 12 AND UP):

TOP WIDTH: 15"

HEIGHT: 16"

BOTTOM WIDTH: 10½"

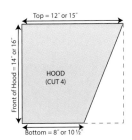

Top = 12" or 15"
Front of Hood = 14" or 16"
HOOD (CUT 4)
Bottom = 8" or 10 ½"

Using a fabric marker and a large rounded object such as a dinner plate as a template, round the right-hand upper corner of the hood shape. The curved edge is the back of the hood and the left-hand, straight side will be the front.

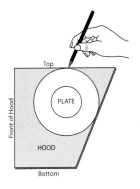

Top
Front of Hood
PLATE
HOOD
Bottom

Cut the shape drawn from both layers to make 2 outer hood pieces. Use these as a template to cut 2 inner hood pieces from the contrasting/lining fabric.

Assemble

*All seams are ½˝. Backstitch at the beginning and end of all seams. No need to finish the seam allowances on this project since there are no exposed seams. When working with laminated cotton, **always** use a pressing cloth, and press from the wrong side whenever possible. Test your iron on a scrap to determine the best settings.*

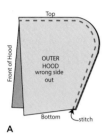

A

1. Place both outer hood pieces right sides together, aligning all raw edges. Pin and stitch up the angled edge, around the rounded corner, and across the top edge to the front of the hood. Leave all other edges unstitched for now. Notch the seam allowance along the curve. Fig. A

2. Repeat Step 1 with the inner hood pieces.

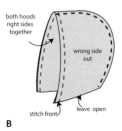

B

3. Place the inner and outer hoods right sides together, with all raw edges and seams aligned, and pin along the straight front edge. Stitch together along the front, leaving the bottom open for turning. Fig. B

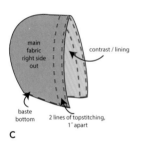

C

4. Turn the hood right side out, and then topstitch along the front edge. For decorative purposes, add a second line of topstitching 1˝ from the first. Baste the bottom edge closed. Fig. C

5. Lay the outer poncho out in a single layer, wrong side up. Mark, pin, or finger-press the halfway points between the center back and center front on the neck opening and the poncho's outer edge. Measure 4˝ out from the neck opening on each side to mark the top of the shoulder with a fabric marker. At the outer edge of the poncho, measure and mark 4˝ to each side of the halfway point. Draw straight lines between the shoulder point and the outer marks to create triangular side darts as shown. Fig. D

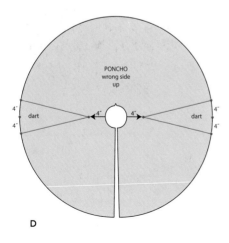

D

6. Fold the poncho in half, right sides together, through the shoulder points, aligning the dart marks. Pin and stitch on the dart lines. Trim the excess fabric ½″ away from the stitching lines and press the seams toward the back. **Fig. E**

7. Repeat Steps 5 and 6 to add darts to the inner poncho.

8. Pin a button placket on a center front edge of the outer/main poncho, right sides together, aligning the raw edges. You can use the matching outer fabric placket or the contrasting placket as photographed. Stitch together along the vertical raw edges. **Fig. F**

9. Press the placket and the seam allowances away from the poncho, and then topstitch the placket close to the seam through all layers. Repeat this step on the other side of the outer poncho and on the inner poncho. **Fig. G**

10. With the outer fabric right sides together, align the back seam of the completed hood with the center back notch on the outer poncho's neck opening. **Fig. H**

Pin the basted edges of the hood to the curved neck opening of the poncho. The front edges of the hood should just meet the 2 button plackets. Baste in place.

11. Place the inner and outer ponchos right sides together, with the hood sandwiched between, and make sure all of the raw edges are perfectly aligned. Pin all around the neck, center front opening, and outer edges. Starting about 2½″ to the left of the center back crease, begin stitching the layers together. Stitch around the bottom edge, up the straight front edge, around the curved neck opening, down the other front edge, and then finally along the bottom edge of the poncho, ending about 5″ away from the starting stitches, leaving a gap for turning. **Fig. I**

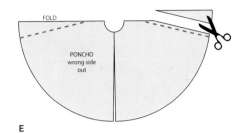

FOLD
PONCHO wrong side out

E

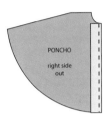

PONCHO right side out

F

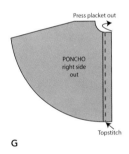

Press placket out
PONCHO right side out
Topstitch

G

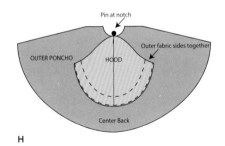

Pin at notch
OUTER PONCHO
HOOD
Outer fabric sides together
Center Back

H

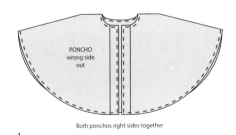

PONCHO wrong side out
Both ponchos right sides together

I

12. Turn the poncho right side out through the opening. Use a blunt object, such as a bone folder or a wooden chopstick, to push out the corners so they are nice and square, and gently tug on the collar to make sure it is pulled out all the way. Topstitch along all of the outer sewn edges, closing the gap. If desired, topstitch again around the outer curve 1″ away from the first line of topstitching for a decorative edge, as you did on the hood.

13. Measure 1″ down from the top of the left button placket as shown and mark the top buttonhole position, centered on the placket. Measure 4″ up from the bottom edge of the placket and mark the bottom buttonhole placement. Measure the distance between the top and bottom markings and divide by 4 (for Girls/Tweens) or 7 (for Women/Teens). Use that number to mark the remaining 3 or 6 buttonhole positions. Create 5 or 7 horizontal buttonholes along the marks, using your button to determine the width.

14. When the buttonholes are finished, align the plackets, placing the right placket under the left, and mark the button placement. Sew the buttons on at the marks. To make the rain poncho fully reversible, sew buttons on the inner side of the placket too. **Fig. J**

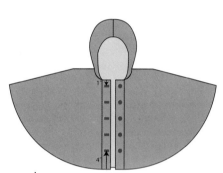

J

VARIATION: Add a cute pocket to the front of the poncho, parallel to the button plackets. Get ideas for cute pockets in Add-Ons (page 131).

> **TIP**
>
> *Practice first on a scrap of fabric to ensure that your buttonhole is big enough for your button. Buttons with a shank are easier to work through the thicker laminated cotton plackets. If yours don't have a built-in shank, you can make one with thread when you sew on the buttons.*

Add-Ons

Add a bit of extra flair to the garments in this book.

These eight mini-projects are designed to embellish and add a bit of extra flair to the garments in this book. Maybe you want to add a belt to your dress or a fun pocket to your top. You will find plenty of optional pieces here to enhance the look of your finished garment.

Braided Fabric Belt

To complete your belt, you will need 2 D-rings 1″ wide or 1 tri-glide buckle 1″ wide. All seams are ½″. Backstitch at the beginning and end of all seams.

1. For the belt, cut 3 strips 2″ by double your Waist measurement.

NOTE

If the cut belt length is longer than the total width of fabric, you may be able to cut the pieces from the length or fabric. Or, for each belt strip, cut 2 equal pieces at half the length calculated + 1″ for seam allowances. Stitch the strips together at a short end and press the seam open.

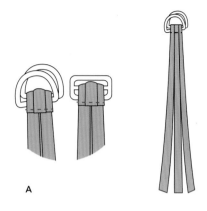

A

2. For the end tab, cut 1 rectangle 2″ × 5″.

3. Fold each of the 3 long strips in half lengthwise right sides together, tucking the short ends in. Press, and then fold the long edges in toward the center crease. Press well, and then topstitch on all 4 sides to create ½″-wide strips with all edges finished.

4. Layer the 3 short ends on top of each other and wrap this end over the flat side of 2 D-rings or the middle bar of a tri-glide buckle. Topstitch across the folded edge. **Fig.A**

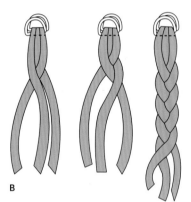

B

5. Braid the strips. Starting with the strips flat, bring the right strip to the middle, then the left strip to the middle, then the right strip again to the middle, and so on. At the end of the braid, overlap all 3 short ends and baste across to keep them together. **Fig.B**

6. Press the 2 short edges of the end tab in ½″ toward the wrong side. Fold the tab in half, right sides together, so the pressed ends are aligned. Stitch a U-shape around the unfinished edges, rounding the corners at the folded end and leaving the pressed edges unstitched for turning. Clip the seam allowance at the corners and turn right side out. Press well. **Fig.C**

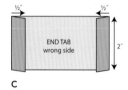

C

END TAB
wrong side

½″   ½″

2″

7. Insert the basted ends of the braided belt inside the end tab. Stitch across the opening of the end tab and all around the perimeter, securing the braided straps inside. **Fig.D**

8. Weave the end tab through the D-rings or tri-glide buckle and cinch the belt tightly around the waist.

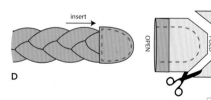

D

insert

OPEN

FOLD

> **TIP**
> *Try this technique with four or five braided strands instead of three for a different look!*

Long Sash

These are perfect to use as belts for dresses or long tunics. Ideally, your sash should be at least twice as long as your Waist circumference. This should allow it to completely wrap around your waist and then tie into a nice bow at the front. If you desire longer bow tails, add length accordingly.

All seams are ½″. Backstitch at the beginning and end of each seam.

1. Cut 1 rectangle for the sash, following these formulas to get the size:

> SASH LENGTH: your Waist measurement × 2, and then add 1″ for seam allowances. Add extra inches, as desired.

> SASH WIDTH: 4″ for all sizes to yield a 1½″-wide sash

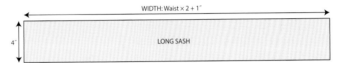

2. Fold the strip right sides together, lengthwise. If you want pointed ends on the sash, stitch the short ends at a 45° angle, and then continue stitching along the length, stopping about halfway through. Leave a 4″–5″ gap for turning, and continue stitching the other side of the sash, pivoting at a 45° angle again at the other short end. If you prefer square ends, stitch straight across each end.

3. Clip the corners and then turn the sash right side out through the opening. Refer to Tools for Sewing (page 14) for information on my favorite turning tool! Use a blunt object, such as a bone folder or a wooden chopstick, to push the points out, and then press well.

4. Topstitch ⅛″ from the finished edge, closing the gap in the process.

5. Wear the sash around your waist with a nice bow tied at the front or side of your body.

NOTE

If your total sash length is longer than the total width of the fabric, you may be able to cut the sash from the length of the fabric. Or cut 2 equal pieces at half the length calculated + 1″ for seam allowances; the seam will be in the center of the sash. Stitch the strips together at a short end and press the seam open.

Basic Patch Pocket

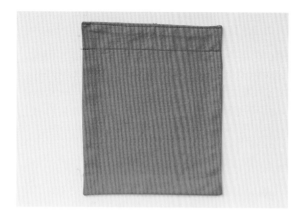

All seams are ½".

1. Determine how wide your pocket should be. It should be at least 2" wider than the width of your hand to allow for ease and seam allowances.

2. For each pocket, cut 2 squares of fabric (or 1 square of main fabric and 1 square of lining) at your hand width measurement + 2".

> **NOTE**
>
> *Start with squares if you want a square pocket. If you want a deeper pocket, cut 2 rectangles the size you would like.*

3. Place the main and lining fabrics right sides together, aligning all raw edges. Stitch around the perimeter of the squares, leaving a small gap at the bottom for turning.

4. Clip the corners within the seam allowance to minimize bulk, and then turn right side out through the opening. Use a turning tool or a blunt tool, such as a bone folder or a wooden chopstick, to push the square corners out. Press well.

5. Topstitch ⅛" from the top edge of the pocket (not the side with the opening), and then again 1" below that to create a decorative edge.

6. Place the pocket on the garment, both with the right side up. It is best to do this while the garment pieces are still flat and not sewn together. Generally, you should place the outer edge of the pocket at least 2" from the garment's side seam and check to be sure you can easily reach the pocket and that it is not positioned too high or too low. Pin the pocket in place and then hold the garment up to yourself or your model to ensure proper placement before stitching it down. Always place pockets straight on the garment, not parallel to the side seams. If your garment has an A-line silhouette, your pockets should be straight, not tilted.

7. When you are happy with the pocket placement, topstitch it to the garment piece, beginning at the top of a side. Stitch a triangle shape at the upper corner to reinforce the stitches. Then stitch down the side, pivot at the bottom corner, and stitch across, closing the gap in the process. Finally, continue to the other upper corner and reinforce that as well, leaving the top edge open.

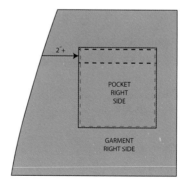

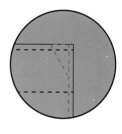

Circular Pocket

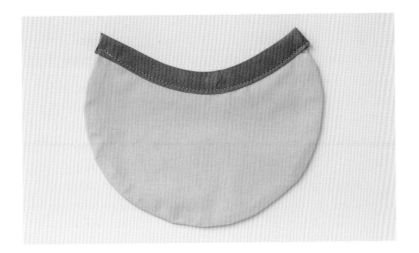

1. Use a medium-sized circular object as a template for your main pocket. Generally, a salad plate will be large enough for most teens and adults. A smaller saucer will work for children. Make sure the circle is at least 2″ wider than the width of your hand.

2. Cut 2 circles of fabric or 1 circle of the main fabric and 1 circle of lining.

3. Place the circles right sides together and pin. Using the same circular template as before, shift the edge of the template about two-thirds of the way up the cut fabric circle to mark the pocket opening. Cut along the opening mark and discard the excess fabric. **Fig. A**

4. Keeping the fabric layers pinned right sides together, stitch along the outer curve, leaving the pocket opening curve unstitched. **Fig. B**

5. Notch the seam allowance all around the outer curve to minimize bulk in the seams, and then turn the pocket right side out through the top opening. Press well, ensuring that the outer curve is nice and smooth.

6. Using a flexible tape measure, measure the total length of the pocket's opening curve. **Fig. C**

For the pocket binding, cut a strip of fabric on the bias 2″ wide × 1″ longer than the pocket opening. Cutting on the bias allows the strip to stretch easily around a curve. **Fig. D**

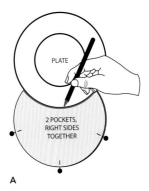

PLATE

2 POCKETS, RIGHT SIDES TOGETHER

A

WRONG SIDE

B

Measure this distance.

RIGHT SIDE

C

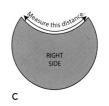

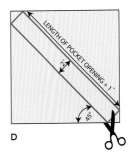

LENGTH OF POCKET OPENING + 1″

45°

D

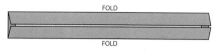

E

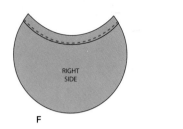

RIGHT SIDE

F

7. Fold the short edges of the binding in ½″ toward the wrong side, and press. Then fold the binding in half lengthwise, wrong sides together, and press to create a crease down the middle. Open the binding, fold the long edges in to meet at the middle crease, and press well. Refold the entire strip to create a ½″-wide double-folded bias tape. **Fig. E**

8. Wrap the binding over the raw edges of the pocket opening, aligning the short folded edges of the binding with the outer edges of the curve. Topstitch close to the inner fold of the binding. **Fig. F**

9. Place the pocket on the right side of the garment, where desired. Refer to Basic Patch Pocket, Steps 6 and 7 (page 134), to find the best pocket placement. Then pin and stitch the outer curved edge of the pocket to the garment. **Fig. G**

Side-Seam Patch Pockets

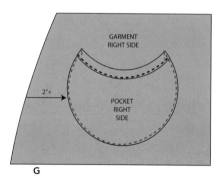

GARMENT RIGHT SIDE

2″+

POCKET RIGHT SIDE

G

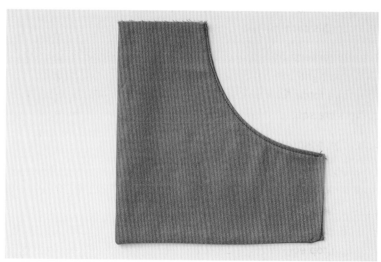

This cute pocket will work on the skirts and pants in this book with side seams. The long side edge of the pocket will be sewn into a vertical seam of the garment.

All seams are ½″. Backstitch at the beginning and end of all seams.

1. Determine how wide your pocket should be. It should be at least 2″ wider than the width of your hand to allow for ease and seam allowances.

2. For each pocket, cut 2 squares of fabric, or 1 square of main fabric and 1 of lining.

NOTE

Start with squares if you want a square pocket. If you want a deeper pocket, cut accordingly.

3. Using a medium-sized circular object (such as a salad plate) as a template, mark a quarter-circle opening on a top corner of the pocket. If you are making a pocket for each side of the garment, cut a mirrored opening on the second pocket. Make sure the opening is large enough for your hand to fit through it. Trim each lining piece to match the corresponding pocket. Fig. A

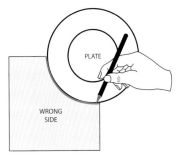

A

> ### TIP
> *To make sure the openings are mirror images, use the first pocket as a template, but place it right sides together with the second pocket.*

4. Place the main pocket and corresponding lining right sides together, aligning all raw edges, and pin. Stitch along the curved pocket opening and any edges that will *not* be sewn into a seam. For a skirt or pants, that would be the bottom edge and long side only, as shown. Leave any edges that will be sewn into a seam open, in this case, the 2 shorter straight edges. Fig. B

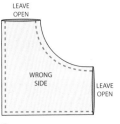

B

Clip the corners within the seam allowance to minimize bulk, and then turn right side out through the opening. Use a blunt tool, such as a bone folder or a wooden chopstick, to make sure the outer corners are square. Press well.

5. Topstitch along the circular opening only. Fig. C

C

6. Position the pocket on the flat garment piece, both right sides up, before the garment has been constructed. Align the open side(s) of the pocket with the edges of the garment piece that will be sewn to another piece. Pin in place. For example, for a skirt or pants, align the open top edge of the pocket with the top edge of the garment (where the waistband will be attached) and the open side with what will be the side seam, as shown.

7. Topstitch along the finished edges, no more than ⅛″ from the edge. Baste the raw edges to the base garment, leaving the curved edge unstitched for the pocket opening. Continue garment construction as indicated. Fig. D

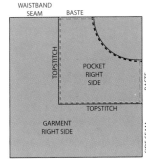

D

Spaghetti Straps

Add these to any of the strapless dresses or tops in this book.

1. Cut 4 strips 1″ × 14″ for Girls/Tweens or 1″ × 18″ for Women/Teens.

TIP

Depending on the width of your fabric, sometimes all four straps will fit in one width of fabric. If they fit, go ahead and cut just a long strip, and do not cut it down to individual size yet. The process will go much faster if you fold, press, and stitch a single piece, and then cut it down to the individual strap length.

---

2. Fold each strap in half lengthwise, wrong sides together. Press, and then open flat.

3. Fold the 2 long edges in toward the wrong side until they meet at the middle crease. Press the edges well.

4. Fold entire piece in half at the crease, encasing the long raw edges. The straps should be ¼″ wide at this point.

5. Topstitch along the long open edge. Leave the 2 short edges unstitched for now.

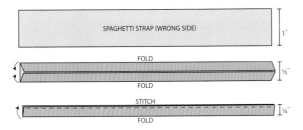

6. Place the finished strapless garment wrong side out on a flat surface. If the garment has 2 seams, the seams should be at the sides. If the garment has a single seam, the seam should be centered at the back. To position the straps, mark the center front and back of the garment, and then measure 2″ to the left and right of the center mark for Girls/Tweens or 3″ to the left and right for Women/Teens. Feel free to adjust these numbers based on your body measurements for a comfortable fit.

7. Fold a short end of each strap over ½″, and then pin each strap to the upper edge of the garment at each mark, so that the folded end is hidden against the wrong side of the garment. Stitch across the strap close to the fold, and then sew a second row of stitches ¼″ away from the first to reinforce.

8. Tie a tight knot at the raw end of each strap.

9. Try the garment on and tie the front and back straps into a bow at the shoulders where comfortable. **Fig. A**

TIP

It helps to pin every few inches to keep the fabric from unfolding as you press these edges, especially when working with knits. If you've assembled a single long strip, cut it into 4 shorter pieces, a piece for each spaghetti strap.

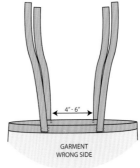

A

Ruffled Hem Band

This band is the perfect embellishment for hems of all the tops, skirts, and dresses in this book. You will need to know the width of the area you are attaching the ruffled band to prior to figuring out measurements for the band. So grab your garment or garment pieces and a tape measure. *Note: All seams are ½˝.*

1. Cut the ruffled band following these formulas to get the size:

LENGTH: 2 × as long as the garment piece to which it will be attached. For example, if your garment is made from 2 panels each 30˝ wide, cut 2 ruffled bands, 60˝ each; if made from a single panel, cut only 1 ruffled band; if already constructed, add 1˝ to the calculated length for seam allowances.

HEIGHT: Variable. Desired finished height + 1˝ for seam and hem allowances.

2. Stitch/serge the band or bands right sides together along the short edges to form a loop.

3. Finish a long edge using your preferred hemming method. I love making a rolled hem with my serger, but a narrow hem will also work well.

4. Sew gathering stitches all the way along the unfinished edge with your longest machine stitch, and leave long thread tails unclipped at the end.

5. Gently pull the bobbin thread to gather the band to half its original length. **Fig. A**

6. Right sides together, pin the gathered edge of the band to the bottom edge of the garment, matching side seams. Stitch together, and then serge or finish the edge. Press the ruffle hem band down and the seam allowance up toward the garment. Topstitch the garment ⅛˝ away from the seam, through all layers. **Fig. B**

NOTE

Don't worry if your calculated ruffled band width is a couple of inches longer than the width of your fabric. Since the band will be gathered and sewn onto the hem later, it is okay if you cut it a bit shorter.

TIP

You may want to stitch separate rows of gathering stitches for the front and the back to prevent thread breakage when pulling.

A

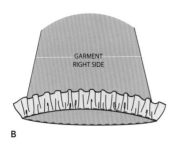

GARMENT
RIGHT SIDE

B

Straight Double-Layer Hem Band

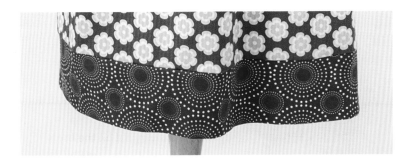

Adding a straight hem band is a great way to add an accent color to your skirt or dress! You will need to know the width of the area you are attaching the hem band to prior to figuring out measurements for the band. So grab your garment or garment pieces and a tape measure.

All seams are ½".

1. Cut the hem band(s) following these formulas to get the size:

LENGTH: The same width as the garment piece(s) to which it will be attached. For example, if your garment is made from 2 panels each 30" wide, make 2 bands 30" wide. If your garment is made up of a single panel, make only 1 hem band.

HEIGHT: Variable. Determine how deep you want the finished band to be. Multiply this number by 2, and then add 1" for seam allowances. For example, for a 3" finished hem band, cut 7" fabric strips.

2. Stitch/serge the band or bands right sides together along the short edges to form a strip. Press seams open.

3. Fold the band lengthwise, wrong sides together, aligning raw edges. Press along the fold to create a crisp crease. **Fig. A**

4. Right sides together, pin the raw edge of the hem band to the bottom edge of the garment, matching side or back seams. Stitch together, and then serge or finish the edge. Press the hem band down and the seam allowances up toward the garment. Topstitch the garment ⅛" away from the seam through all the layers. **Fig. B**

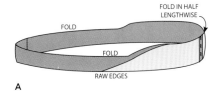

A

B

About the Author

Patty Young grew up in San José, Costa Rica, in an environment where she was encouraged to express her creativity freely. Both of her parents dabbled in the arts, so it was only natural that she would inherit their creative genes. They moved to the United States in 1987, and Patty attended the University of Central Florida, where she received her bachelor of fine arts degree in graphic design and photography.

Over the next twelve years, Patty honed her graphic design skills at a couple of marketing agencies before deciding to leave her corporate job in 2005 to stay home with her children and pursue her own creative endeavors.

Today, Patty owns and operates MODKID LLC and serves in the role of lead designer. MODKID specializes in high-quality boutique-style sewing patterns for children's and women's clothes, doll clothes, purses, and other assorted accessories and home furnishings. Patty also designs textiles, ribbons, scrapbooking papers, die-cutting shapes, and many other craft-related products for such companies as Riley Blake Designs, Jo-Ann Fabric and Craft Stores, Momenta, and Silhouette America.

To learn more about Patty and what she's cooking up next, please visit her at her popular blog, modkidboutique.blogspot.com, and feel free to leave a comment. She would love to hear from you!

ALSO BY PATTY YOUNG:

Resources

The fabrics and trims shown in this book are courtesy of...

Jo-Ann Fabric and Craft Stores   joann.com

Chiffons, matte jerseys, cotton eyelets, tulle, ribbons, elastics, buttons, and trims

Riley Blake Designs   rileyblakedesigns.com

Quilting cottons, knits, canvas, and laminates

Shannon Fabrics   shannonfabrics.com

Cuddle, Cuddle Suede, and Silky Satin